CASTLES&
PALACES
OF EUROPE

METRO BOOKS
New York

An Imprint of Sterling Publishing Co., Inc.
1166 Avenue of the Americas
New York, NY 10036

Original publication © 2002 DuMont monte Verlag, Cologne, Germany
Revised edition © 2017 Rebo International b.v., The Netherlands

ISBN 978-1-4351-6652-3

For information about custom editions, special sales, and premium and corporate purchases, please contact Sterling Special Sales at 800-805-5489 or specialsales@sterlingpublishing.com.

Manufactured in Slovakia

2 4 6 8 10 9 7 5 3

www.sterlingpublishing.com

Credits: Cover design by 100%Creatief, The Netherlands; Photo Credits – see page 416

CASTLES&
PALACES
OF EUROPE

ULRIKE SCHÖBER

METRO BOOKS
New York

CONTENTS

INTRODUCTION

Fortress, castle, palace, chateau – these terms immediately conjure up associations, pictures and images from our childhood and fairytales, from Hollywood films and from our dreams. They give rise to new images and terms that flow like an inexhaustible spring: battlements, towers and drawbridges, cannons, bastions, knights and armor, stucco and marble, flights of steps and gardens. Imagination knows no bounds and tends to link terms that do not belong together. Romantic knights and castles from the age of chivalry soon merge with the lavish magnificence of a lordly palace. The mind's eye often creates impressions that have little in common with reality.

This book will bring fortresses, castles and palaces back into the world of reality. It will acquaint us with architectural developments and styles, illustrated by carefully selected examples. It introduces us to extraordinary buildings and evokes the clammy coldness within those thick walls. It reminds us that baroque architecture was also a claim to power and reflected a conception of oneself.

But above all, this book should awaken your interest in castles and palaces. It should encourage you to go on a short holiday and visit a castle or fortress. It might also encourage you to visit some old castle ruins or a manor house that may not be as famous as the ones described in this book, but will nevertheless have much in common with them. It should also make you aware not only of famous sights but also of your own surroundings and encourage you to look at architecture with a fresh eye, open to new developments and styles because architecture always reflects people and their epoque, which is why castles, palaces and country houses are so important.

Power architecture through the ages

Castles were typically constructed to represent medieval power, not only in Europe but also in the Byzantine Empire. In the late Middle Ages over 30,000 castles and fortresses were built to reinforce the aristocracy's claims to power. The history of castle and fortress building changed continuously to adapt to developments in the field of weaponry that in turn enabled rulers to expand their territory.

◀ **LEFT**
Medieval castles, like Coca Castle in Spain, served as a demonstration of power and they also had a defensive function. They had to be extended constantly to keep up with the development of offensive weapons

Right
An example of
a historic castle
complex: Burg Eltz in
the Rheine valley ▶

The constant improvement of weapons during the 14th century, in particular the invention of gunpowder, resulted in many castles being abandoned as residences and allowed to fall into disrepair because they were no longer secure. Other castles were fortified and turned into fortresses or enlarged as a statement of power. In the latter case, these were no longer used to defend territories but were an expression of self-importance on the part of the ruler who considered his position secure and wanted to display his power through an imposing building. The highpoint of this display of splendor and power was without any doubt to be found in the absolutism of Louis XIV, whose palace at Versailles was the most striking expression of this tendency.

When the political power of the European aristocracy became eroded by the growth of democracy in the 19th century, smaller, traditional, stately homes were built again. Having lost their defensive role, castles now also lost their status. Most individual monarchs no longer had the absolute power that they had once expressed with such splendor and magnificence. Interestingly, even when the move to democracy seemed to proceed at different speeds and in different ways in the various European countries, the impact on the building of castles and palaces was the same everywhere.

The castles and fortresses of the 19th century were the romantic result of a revival of medieval chivalry and an idealized view of castle architecture. They were now products of historicism that borrowed features from past architectural styles according to taste without considering their own innate necessity and function. They have very little in common with the real castles of the Middle Ages.

The castle as an instrument of defense

The predecessors of European castles were mottes. This is the term used to describe the wooden tower castles built between the 8th and 11th centuries. They were built either directly on a hill or rocky outcrop, or on a man-made mound of earth. (The word motte comes from the Latin mutta and the French motte, meaning a mound.) The tower had a raised entrance so that the occupants could barricade themselves inside, and a projecting top floor and was additionally enclosed by a protective wooden palisade. Attackers had to first climb the steep hill or mound, a feat that quickly exhausted them. They then had to face the well-rested

◀ **LEFT**
In the construction
of Festung Munot in
Schaffhausen, Albrecht
Durer's theory of
fortification
was followed. The
circular fortress meant
that all-round defence
was possible

defenders in the tower and engage in hand-to-hand sword fighting. Because the mottes were made of wood and therefore flammable, and since they failed of provide sufficient protection from increasingly effective weapons, very few traces of these mottes remain in Europe.

The motte was gradually replaced by a simple rectangular stone building that had only a raised entrance and often a defensive wall on the side that was most at risk. But by the beginning of the 12th century, these early fortresses were no longer sufficient for defense.

This marked the beginning of the era of the traditional medieval castle, built according to a tried and tested formula adapted to local topographical conditions and regional requirements. Each fortress had fortifications and residential quarters as well as domestic and farm buildings.

The first stage in effective defense was the choice of a site. Wherever possible castles were built on an almost inaccessible mountain or a rocky outcrop. They were visible from a distance and difficult to capture. This in itself expressed the occupant's claim to power in the region. The counterparts of these hilltop castles were the lowland castles built in the plains. Ditches, embankments and walls or wide moats such as those found in moated castles such as Wasserschloss Raesfeld provided protection (page 74).

A feature common to nearly all castles was the keep, and larger castles might have two keeps. This main tower also served as a lookout post and a last refuge against attack, but not as a residence. At best, it had one room with a fireplace for the guards and a lavatory. The raised entrance of the keep was reached by means of a wooden ladder or wooden bridge, or, very rarely, by stone stairs, so that enemies could easily be prevented from entering. Usually this tower was made from undressed stone or simple stone blocks and was located in the most vulnerable part of the castle, or in the center, with walls 5 to 10 ft thick.

A high ring wall protected the fortress, which was made more secure by additional watchtowers that guarded the unprotected parts of the castle such as the gates and the weaker sides. Special gate towers were linked to the gate and were frequently equipped with machicolations through which stones, boiling oil or pitch could be poured onto the attackers, as well as water to put out fires if the wooden gates were set alight by the enemy. Many gate towers also had battlements. If the castle was surrounded by a ditch or was inaccessible because of a crevice in the rock, the drawbridge provided additional security.

Hilltop fortresses on rocky plateaus were built for topographical reasons in such a way that the walls of the outer buildings already provided protection. On the other hand, lowland castles nearly always had an additional ring of walls. Almost all of them had battlements that protected the guards to chest height, and a sentry walk to defend the walls from the top. In many cases, the two were combined. Often wooden planks that could be raised were installed between the battlements so that the attacker could not see inside the castle, and also to prevent projectiles from landing inside the castle. In addition, there were crenellations in the walls and towers through which the castle could be defended. Bows and crossbows, arquebuses and cannons could be fired through these openings. Their exact size and shape depended on the weapons that were intended to be used.

The domestic and farm buildings were seldom built from the same stone blocks as the walls, towers and residential quarters; they were usually constructed from undressed stone, boulders, pebbles or half-timbering because these materials were less costly.

The most important requirement for the inhabitants of a fortress was a reliable source of water, ideally one that could not be cut off by the enemy during a siege. If there was no spring, a cistern was installed. In addition, the castle also included storerooms, stables, workshops and a kitchen that, depending on the size of the castle, was housed in a separate building or in special rooms.

In the center of castle were the residential quarters that, depending on the size of the complex but also on the period when it was built, were conceived as a donjon or great hall. The term donjon or keep refers to a tower-shaped building that could also be used for defensive purposes, but (unlike the earlier keeps) it was inhabited all the time and was larger and more comfortable as a result. The donjon was an earlier, more modest variation of the great hall. The ground floor almost always contained storerooms and, like the keep, the entrance was on the first floor where the main heated room with wall seats could also be found. The chapel was on the same floor or on the floor above. The unheated bedrooms were on the floor above that. It is hard to imagine how bitterly cold these castles must have been in winter.

The high aristocracy often added a great hall to the castle complex that was larger than a donjon and served no protective

Right
In spite of its situation in the impassable Pyrenees, the Cathar fortress of Quéribus could not withstand a siege indefinitely ▶

function. But this too was very cold because the walls were 3 to 5 ft thick and were frequently provided with ornate arched windows overlooking the inner courtyard. Outside stairs led to the entrance on the first floor that opened onto a spacious, heated room used as an official reception room but, more importantly, as a dining room for the lords of the castles and the servants. The ground floor usually contained the storerooms as well as the kitchen and the stables. Many castles with a great hall also had a separate chapel and a separate building for the living and sleeping quarters.

Most important castles developed from this typical plan because they were rarely built entirely from scratch. Instead, the aristocracy preferred to enlarge their family seat to display their power, or to extend another castle that had been given to them as a fief.

In the 13th century, a new kind of throwing device – the trebuchet – was invented that enabled large stones or boulders to be hurled a long distance. This made it possible for attackers to make breaches in the defensive walls and thus to enter the castle. In order improve their defense, fortresses were surrounded by a second ring of walls, thus creating a kind of corridor. Thus if the attackers managed to get over the first ring of walls, they were exposed to the firepower of the occupants of the fortress while trying to climb over the inner wall ring. In peacetime, the space between the two rings of walls was used for tournaments, as an animal enclosure and even as a vegetable garden.

As firearms gradually became more widespread, space had to be made for them so that they could be used effectively. For instance, bulwarks, bastions or entrenchments were built in front of the fortification walls where heavy cannons were placed. In this way, the sides of the fortress were protected. The cumbersome, old watchtowers were pulled down. The Belgian chateau of Bouillon is a perfect example of this development (page 204).

As a result, many existing castles were enlarged and altered to meet new defensive require-

ments. It was extremely rare that rulers built fortresses in strategic sites specially to extend their sphere of influence. The main difference between a fortress and castle is that fortresses were used exclusively for defense purposes. Soldiers were housed in fortresses and the comfort level was low. Moreover, they were useless in peacetime and their maintenance was expensive. As a result of the developments in weapon technology, fortress construction became an architectural discipline in its own right and fortresses were built exclusively to achieve the best results for defense purposes.

◀ **LEFT**
With the invention of firearms, cannon entrenchments were added to defensive castle installations

The castle as a synthesis of the arts

The development of firearms marked a turning point in the history of castles and fortresses. No longer secure, many of them were abandoned and allowed to fall into disrepair. Alternatively, they were enlarged and converted into imposing, aristocratic residences or seats of government for religious or secular rulers. The construction of new castles started with the Renaissance in the 16th century.

Architects were still influenced by the castles of the past and the various buildings were arranged around an interior courtyard. The parts of the building were subordinated to a master plan and built in a regular shape, often on a rectangular ground plan. The layout was often symmetrical. Large complexes consisting of four wings such as Schloss Johannisburg (page 38) were rare. Living quarters, farm buildings and official apartments were often in separate buildings or wings. Banqueting rooms and private apartments were usually on the first floor and accessible through a spiral staircase.

After the Thirty Years War (1619–48) absolutism developed and the Baroque castle became the typical feudal construction. Monarchs and princes were above the law and had virtually unlimited power that was only restricted by religion, natural law and Basic Law. The central concept was the sovereignty embodied in the three-part Baroque castles of the 17th and 18th century. All the axes of the various buildings and garden converged on the central building and ideally they were symmetrical mirror images of each other. This concept was most clearly applied in the hunting lodge of Stupinigi (page 350). However, the real prototype was the vast, unrivaled palace of Versailles, created by Louis XIV (page 192).

Baroque palaces are one of the highpoints of European architecture because they were conceived as a synthesis of the arts, something that had been previously been impossible financially. Absolutism was the quintessential autocratic form of goverment because it encouraged the monarch to invest his fortune and that of his people in building an imposing castle that would reflect his central dominant, position.

After the French Revolution throughout Europe absolute monarchy was gradually replaced by liberal constitutions, and during the classical period, only a small number of castles were built from scratch, such as Schloss Wilhelmshöhe in Kassel (page 102).

The historicism of the 19th century combined all the architec-

RIGHT
The Doge's Palace in Venice was originally a defensive castle and eventually became the palace of the great maritime trading power's government ▶

tural styles of previous periods. As well as sumptuous historical castles, there were others inspired by the idealized concept of the medieval castle, but since they were residences they were decorated and furnished in a lavish manner, such as Schloss Neuschwanstein (page 60).

Nowadays few castles or palaces are still used as seats of parliament or for official royal duties in the manner of the Royal Palace in Madrid (page 390). Nor are the palaces inhabited by royal families necessarily the most beautiful or architecturally outstanding in the country. Buckingham Palace, for example is not in this book, but Hampton Court Palace is.

Today smaller palaces or country houses are frequently inhabited by the descendants of the former ruling classes. They often find it difficult to maintain these buildings since being the owner of a castle or stately home can be an expensive pleasure. As a result, more and more owners open their doors to the public, organizing tours and offering other attractions.

The largest and most important castles and palaces are all open to the public as cultural and historical monuments. They are popular tourist destinations, which means they can be crowded in the high season, and to visit them all would involve a prodigious amount of traveling. When an actual visit is undesirable or impossible, this book may be an excellent substitute.

RIGHT
With time, the ability of castles and palaces to impress became more important than any defensive function ▶

Schloss Augustusburg

Clemens Augustus, Archbishop and Elector of Cologne, believed that each activity or occupation needed an appropriate setting reflecting its importance. He built the imposing Baroque castle of Augustusburg in Brühl and also a hunting lodge, Schloss Falkenlust, at the far end of the park. Together the castle, the hunting lodge and the gardens form one of the most magnificent Baroque ensembles in Germany, one that has been listed by UNESCO as a World Cultural and Natural Heritage Site.

When looking for a site for his new court, Clemens Augustus (1700–61) was immediately taken by the beauty of Brühl in the Rhineland and its suitable location for falconry. He disliked living and ruling in the Bonn residence of his predecessor. He wanted a residence fit for a prince where he could fulfill his duties as a ruler and indulge his passion for falconry. The architect Johann Conrad Schlaun drew up plans for a moated castle based on the Westphalian model and the first stone was laid in 1725. Parts of the ruins of an ancient fortress were included and the horseshoe-shaped shell of the building was ready after three years. At this point Augustus called upon the Bavarian court architect François de Cuvilliés and entrusted the interior decoration of the building to him. Schlaun was dismissed.

Cuvilliés made considerable changes to Schlaun's plans because his ideas for the interior decoration of the castle required certain alterations to the building itself. The towers and the moat disappeared and two long galleries were added to the west. Only the east facade with wings designed by Schlaun have survived.

On entering the building, the visitor is immediately faced with a masterpiece: the magnificent staircase made by Balthasar Neumann between 1743 and 1748, a real Rococo gem created as a tribute to his patron Clemens Augustus. It is impossible to miss the Elector's gilded bust, or his initials, CA, which appear everywhere. Carlo Carlone painted the ceiling above the staircase to simulate a copola. Two double flights of stairs lead in a bold sweep to the first floor where the living quarters of the prince are situated in the north wing and the large state rooms in the west wing. These are wonderfully decorated with stucco, marble, gilded features, superb painted ceilings, heavy chandeliers, tapestries, selected pieces of furniture and fine

RIGHT
The staircase designed by Balthasar Neumann with the painted ceiling by Carlo Carlone ▶

FOLLOWING DOUBLE SPREAD
View of the east front of Schloss Augustusburg with the court of honor ▶▶

◀ **LEFT**
Sculptured figures supporting the staircase

parquet floors. Everywhere there are elegant objects and designs to impress visitors and provide a suitable setting for the prince after whom Schloss Augustusburg is named. The decoration of the guardroom was inspired by the royal house of Wittelsbach. In the large banqueting hall the Elector is celebrated by Apollo and the muses and elevated to the summit of creation. A look through the tall windows into the Baroque gardens confirms the power of man to bring order to nature. The gardens were originally laid out by Dominique Girard, a pupil of the famous landscape gardener André Le Nôtre. In the 19th century they were redesigned by Peter Josef Lenné in the English landscape style popular at the time. But during the last century, they were restored to the original layout of 1750 so as to re-establish the overall Rococo impression. Only the summerhouses were not rebuilt.

The longest avenue in the garden of Schloss Augustusburg leads to Schloss Falkenlust. This building, erected by François de Cuvilliés between 1729 and 1733, is fairly intimate compared to the palatial main building and was used more often by the Elector. There he indulged his passion for falconry with a few select guests, small parties waited on by only a few servants. It was here too that he retreated with his mistresses. Falkenlust was also much more convenient than Augustusburg for secret political meetings.

The staircase in this smaller building is an artistic treasure well worth seeing. Its walls are decorated with some 10,000 blue and white tiles depicting falconry scenes, specially commissioned by Clemens Augustus for this staircase. Equally fine are the Chinese lacquer panels in the small room known as the "cabinet".

There is a falconry museum in one of the side wings of the castle, a reminder of the prince's passion for falconry.

◄ **LEFT**
Beautifully painted ceiling in one of the rooms of the Augustusburg

The Schlosskirche

The former cloister-church of the Franciscans of 1493 was modernized by Elector Clemens Augustus in 1735. As a connecting section between the simple single-nave building and the palace, an orangery with a two-story oratory and a tripartite enclosed choir was built. Delightfully ornamented with charming side chapels and pointed arches beneath cross-rib vaults, the high altar of marble- like colored stucco is a masterpiece of Balthasar Neumann (1745), filling the whole height of the choir to the ceiling vault. The sculptures were made by the Würzburg sculptor Johann Wolfgang von der Auvera.

Burg Eltz

"The solitude and beauty of the place appeals greatly to the imagination – Burg Eltz is the epitome of how a castle should look." This is how the eminent art critic Georg Dehio described the castle and its many turrets, a building that incorporates 500 years of castle architecture.

Burg Eltz is situated between Cochem and Coblenz in the Rhine valley. Built in picturesque surroundings on a rocky outcrop, it guards the steep-sided Elzbach valley of the Moselle river. The castle has been the property of the noble von Eltz family for over 800 years and is still maintained by the family's private funds. Unlike other castles in similar surroundings, it has never been destroyed or plundered in its long history, so it provides a true picture of architectural history and interior design in Germany.

The castle's delightful charm lies in its intricate turrets, towers and various floors. The living quarters are in eight towers with steeply pitched roofs and there are numerous little pointed turrets made of undressed stone and half-timbering. All the parts are so closely interconnected that at first glance it is hard to tell where one starts and the other ends. Throughout its 500 year building history, which merged Romanesque, Gothic, Renaissance and early Baroque style, a harmonious ensemble has emerged. This is no romantic, staged product of an individual's imagination, like for instance the fairy-tale castle of Neuschwanstein (see page 60). It is a castle that has grown organically throughout history to meet the requirements of

the von Eltz family. Indeed, the history of the Burg Eltz and the family have always been closely linked.

In 1157, Emperor Frederick I, known as Barbarossa, presented the ancient fortress to Rudolf von Eltz the elder as a gift. Surrounded on three sides by the Elzbach, the late-Romanesque Platt-Eltz keep and remains of the Romanesque dwelling dating from that period are still preserved in the basement of the Kempenich building.

In the mid–13th century, the castle and estate was divided between the brothers Elias, Wilhelm and Theodorich. From that time, Burg Eltz became a Ganerbenburg in which several branches of the von Eltz family lived as a Ganerbengemeinschaft, a kind of medieval group sharing the castle and organized according to fixed rules. The rights and obligations of the castle inhabitants as well as the maintenance and administration of the castle were all laid down in "keep letters". Individual family branches lived and worked separately in their respective "living towers", sharing certain parts of the castle such as

Right
View of the castle gateway and its tall, prominent residential towers ▶

◀ **Left**
Ceiling of 1520 in the bedchamber of the Rübenacher House

the courtyard, the well, the chapel and the assembly hall.

The peace and quiet of this family community was rudely disturbed in 1331 when the von Eltz lords joined other knights of the realm to oppose the territorial policies of the Elector Balduin. He built a fortress, Trutz- or Baldeneltz Burg, on a rocky outcrop on the opposite side of the valley from where he laid siege to Burg Eltz. The ruins of Balduin's fortress are still visible in the forest where they are slowly becoming overgrown. From that vantage point, he set about besieging the members of the von Eltz family in their own dwelling. Firearms were not yet available, but Balduin attacked Burg Eltz by catapulting huge boulders. The siege lasted two years until the knights of Eltz eventually surrendered in 1336 and made peace.

A few boulders can still be seen in the courtyard of Burg Eltz, recalling the only military event in the history of the castle. Apart from this brief warlike interlude, the von Eltz family has always either avoided disputes or solved them through diplomacy. For instance, Hans Anton zu Eltz-Üttingen, who served as a high-ranking officer in the French army, succeeded in saving the castle from destruction during the Palatine War of Succession.

When building the castle, the von Eltz knights took the geographical conditions of the site, a rocky outcrop 230 ft high, into account. An oval plateau built on top of the outcrop forms the ground plan of the fortress. At times, up to a hundred family members were housed in this relatively small space. For this reason, an outer surrounding fortress was built, composed of individual buildings set so close together that their back walls acted as defenses.

Erected in 1472, the Rübenach building with its multi-angled, half-timbered turret, its simple projecting oriel resting on two basalt columns above the entrance door and its late Gothic chapel oriel window, dominates the architectural diversity of the castle's inner courtyard. The Rodendorfer buildings were erected between 1490 and 1540. A vaulted porch, supported by three pillars, adorns the facade overlooking the courtyard. The outer wall is embellished with a mosaic depicting the Madonna, dating from the previous century. The interior gives a lively impression of life in the past.

The treasures of Burg Eltz

The treasures of Burg Eltz are in the cellar vaults of the Rübenacher House. Here, there is a varied art collection with over 500 exhibits from the 12th to the 19th century which any museum would be proud to own. Beside masterpieces of the goldsmith's and silversmith's art, there are collections of Hoechst and Viennese porcelain from the 18th century, as well as curiosities such as "Gluttony displayed by Drunkenness". All the exhibits belonged to members of the von Eltz family and were usually acquired for everyday use.

◀ **LEFT**
The inner courtyard
of the castle

Heidelberger Schloss

"Ruins that soar into the sky are especially beautiful on clear days when the scudding clouds part the windows or high above them can be seen. Their destruction reinforces the eternity of these ruins through the transient spectacle that they reveal to the skies."
(Walter Benjamin, Heidelberger Schloss)

The view of the imposing Heidelberger Schloss from the mighty bridge across the Neckar river is world-famous. Surrounded by woodland, the castle dominates the river and the old town below it. The most beautiful castle ruins in Germany continue to fascinate and attract people from all over the world, evoking the emotions expressed by Walter Benjamin's words. Epitomizing German romanticism, the ruins of Heidelberger Schloss still attract countless visitors every year and it is one of the essential stopping-places for tourists visiting Germany. The castle ruins are also used as a stage setting every year in August when plays and concerts are organized in the context of the famous castle festival. These events have their origin in choral and serenade concerts first held in 1837 and they take place in the courtyard, surrounded by nine palace buildings.

The castle has had a turbulent history that is reflected in the buildings of the various periods.

As a medieval fortress in the 13th century, it guarded the Neckar valley and especially the crossing to the Schönau monastery. In the late 15th and early 16th centuries, Frederick I and Ludwig I built fortifications with four massive, round towers – necessary because of the progress of weapons technology. In the 16th and 17th centuries the imperial rulers gave free rein to their passion for building and added palatial buildings in Renaissance style, the Ottheinrichsbau and the Fried richsbau, so that the fortress became a magnificent castle.

Frederick V completed the castle by erecting buildings in the English style above the fortifications to the west, surrounded by magnificent gardens that are famous throughout Europe.

Large parts of the castle were destroyed by the French during the War of the League of Augsburg (1688-97). The efforts of Elector Karl Theodor to rebuild the castle were thwarted by nature when it was struck by lightning and large parts of the structure destroyed in 1764. Heidelberg Schloss has been a ruin ever since and different epoques have interpreted the fact differently. In the 19th century, it became a nationalist symbol after its destruction

RIGHT
Main facade of the Friederichsbau ▶

FOLLOWING DOUBLE SPREAD
View of Heidelberger Schloss from the opposite bank of the Neckar. As well as the surviving bell tower and Frederichsbau, there are the ruins of the main keep and the Englische Bau ▶▶

◀ **LEFT**
Figures on the facade refer to the original defensive function of the castle

by the French, while German romantic poets saw the ruins as a symbol of the transience of man and of earthly power.

Compared with many other ruins, there is still much to be seen here because parts of the castle have been rebuilt. The Ottheinrich building on the east side of the castle courtyard is recognized as one of the most important buildings of the early Renaissance and its facade is adorned with statues in the Italian style. The height of its floors increases with each story, so that the building appears taller than it actually is. In the basement is the Apothekenmuseum (Pharmacy Museum) with fourteen rooms illustrating the development of medicine from ancient alchemy to modern pharmaceuticals. The exhibits include ancient jars, pots, pestles and presses as well as cupping glasses and enema syringes.

The Friedrichs building on the north side of the courtyard illustrates the further stylistic development of the period, reflected in the wealth of details typical of the late Renaissance. The sixteen statues on the facade represent ancestors of the Wittelbach family. A balcony higher up overlooking the Neckar provides a magnificent view of Heidelberg and the Neckar valley. Parts of the castle church on the ground floor are Gothic but the altar dates from the beginning of the 18th century. It is a popular venue for stylish wedding ceremonies – but only if the couple is happy to share the occasion with the public. When they pose for the official wedding photograph on leaving the church, the newly-weds will be greeted and photographed not only by their friends and relatives but also by the many tourists who are fascinated to come upon such a romantic Heidelberg scene.

The Heidelberger Fass

The vast Heidelberger Fass or barrel was accommodated in a special cellar in the Englische Bau by Elector Karl Theodor in 1751. It is 30 ft long, 26 ft high and 23 ft wide, making it for a long time the largest barrel of this kind in the world. It can hold about 50,000 gallons of wine, enough for the annual tithe of one-tenth of the Palatinate vintage, the share to which the elector was entitled at that time. Karl Theodor was obviously a wine enthusiast, but he was also a practical man. He had the Fass connected directly to the main hall with a pump and measuring equipment. On some days, as many as 450 gallons of wine were drawn from the barrel.

◀ **LEFT**
The most beautiful
castle ruins in Germany

Burg Hohenzollern

"The prospect from Burg Hohenzollern is really worth a journey", said Kaiser Wilhelm II when visiting the castle. The view stretches from the Swabian Alps and the Black Forest to the Swiss Alps in the distance. Burg Hohenzollern is one of the most important German national monuments of the 19th century.

Not only is the view from Burg Hohenzollern spectacular, but the view of the castle is equally splendid. Situated south of Tübingen, its towers, turrets, pointed roofs and gables crown the Zoller mountain after which it is named. It owes its present form to King Friedrich Wilhelm IV, who had it built between 1850 and 1867 as a last, glorious, and defiant gesture of the monarchy in the face of Parliamentarianism.

He had visited the ruins of his ancestral home in 1819 as Crown Prince and it was then that he had the idea of awakening the castle, like Sleeping Beauty, from its long sleep. After all, the history of his family, a royal and ruling house of ancient lineage, was contained within its walls. The first castle on the Zoller was built in 1061. It is from this mountain that the Hohenzollern family derives its name, since it was customary in those days to take your name from where you lived. In 1423, the castle, then in the hands of the robber baron of Zollern, was destroyed by the Swabian league towns and King Sigmund issued a decree, whereby it was banned "in perpetuity" from being rebuilt. The ban was lifted just 30 years later by Kaiser Friedrich III, when the castle was in fact rebuilt on an even bigger and grander scale. It was expanded into a fortress between 1617 and 1633. From 1771 on, however, after the withdrawal of the Austrians, who had captured and occupied it in the meantime, the castle fell into disrepair – until the Crown Prince, now King Friedrich Wilhelm IV, was able to fulfill the dream of his youth and demonstrate to the proponents of democracy just what a monarchy is capable of.

The ground plan of the ancient Burg Hohenzollern, as well as a few additional buildings, such as St. Michael's Chapel, the Bishop's Tower, the Kaiser Tower, and Markgrafen Tower, were incorporated into the new edifice. The soaring architectural features which give the castle such a distinctive appearance from afar, were new additions, however. They were intended to create the image of an idyllic knight's castle in tune with Romantic, 19th century ideals, and could not fail to impress would-be democrats. Prince Louis Ferdinand of Prussia (1907-1994) saw to it that the castle became as much of a showpiece on the inside as it was externally. He was a collector of valuable objets d'art and examples of Prussian history, from paintings through furniture to the military uniform of Friedrich The Great. The rooms of the castle, with their marble columns, painted and coffered ceilings, elegant wall hangings, and woodpaneled walls provide a perfect setting for these treasures.

Right
With marble columns, painted ceilings and elegant wallpapers, the richly decorated rooms of the castle display exhibits relating to the history of Prussia ▶

Following double spread
The 19th century image of an idealized knightly castle became a reality with the building of Burg Hohenzollern ▶▶

SCHLOSS JOHANNISBURG

Schloss Johannisburg in Aschaffenburg is one of the largest four-sided castles of the Renaissance. With its harmonious style and beautiful location on the bank of the Main River, it is a very attractive building of red sandstone, overlooking a beautiful park on the other bank.

In 1552, a large fire destroyed most of the town of Aschaffenburg in Bavaria and also its medieval castle. As a result, the Archbishop-Elector Johann Schweickard von Kronberg commissioned the Strasbourg architect Georg Ridinger to build a new castle. He designed a harmonious, almost symmetrical building, arranged on a square ground plan with four three-storied wings enclosing a square courtyard. The corner towers, also square, project a little beyond the facade and define the wings while conferring a decidedly majestic character on the castle. The harmony is broken only by the old keep in the inner courtyard which Ridinger had preserved from the ruins of the fire, that is not exactly in the center of the north wing but slightly displaced to the east.

The exterior facades of the wings are sober, decorated only by the regular arrangement of the superimposed windows and dormer windows, and the horizontal stringcourses that fol-

low the division into three floors. The gable in the center of each wing adds a touch of variety, breaking the line of the pitched roof. The upper part is graduated in three steps, and embellished with windows decorated in the Mannerist style. They carry the eye to the rooftops of the corner towers and the keep that are embellished in a similar style and become even more ornate towards the top. Above the seventh floor the corner towers become octagonal, thus giving an impression of roundness. They are surmounted by domed roofs with lanterns made from slate. The keep, on the other hand, is covered with a steep, hipped roof with small, round, pointed towers at the corners.

The chapel is neatly integrated within the north wing of the castle. The marble and alabaster altar was created by Hans Junker; it contains a wealth of detail, including a depiction of the architect with a model of the building on the right.

The west wing contains official rooms and a picture gallery. The fine interior decoration was commissioned by the Elector Frederick Karl von Erthal who ruled from 1774 until 1802. It has been very carefully restored so that the rooms give a perfect im-

RIGHT
The symmetrical early 17th century design is clearly visible in the tower behind the medieval keep ▶

FOLLOWING DOUBLE SPREAD
Set on an enormous plinth, the three-storied building rises high above the bank of the Main River ▶▶

◀ **LEFT**
The altar of the Schlosskirche with its alabaster figures is a fine example of 17th century sculpture

pression of early German classicism. The gallery houses an exhibition of paintings from Bavarian state collections with some important works by artists such as Hans Baldung Grien and Lucas Cranach. The castle library in the northwest corner tower has some valuable early printed works and manuscripts from Mainz, although these are not always on show.

Schloss Johannisburg is situated on the Main River, but it is raised up above the shore to prevent it from being flooded when the water rises. To achieve this, the architect Ridinger considerably enlarged the terrace of the old castle, which is supported by a massive wall that is well above the high water mark. It was on this secure terrace that the castle was built. From the sumptuous rooms of the west wing, the view stretches across the river to the magnificent Schönbusch park on the far side. This English-style garden was commissioned by the Elector Frederick Karl von Erthal. The gardens were designed by the Portuguese architect Emmanuel Joseph d'Herigoyen and later laid out by Frederick Ludwig Sckell, while the Portuguese architect concentrated on the buildings in the park.

The best known and oldest building in the Schönbusch park is the Schlösschen or "little castle". Built in classical style, it has two floors with an attic floor above them. The facade is fairly sober, punctuated only by doors and windows, and the interior decoration is not particularly lavish, expressing restrained elegance reminiscent of ancient Greece and Rome. The Friendship temple, built in 1800, is also built in the classical style. In contrast, the "Dörfchen" or "little village", built in 1788, consists of several "romantic" houses that create an aristocratic country idyll, gentle and carefree.

The Fascination with ancient Rome

Between 1830 and 1840, Kaiser Ludwig I of Bavaria was spending more and more time at Aschaffenburg. There he commissioned the building of a house in the "classical" style, inspired by the House of Castor and Pollux excavated in Pompeii. This "Pompeianum" was to contain objects that would have been found in an ancient Roman house. During 1840–48, Frederick von Gärtner built the king a house in classical Roman style with columns and mosaics, a romantic folly on a rocky outcrop overlooking a vineyard. Pompeii itself had been buried by a thick layer of ashes during the eruption of Vesuvius in 79 AD and rediscovered in 1748, whereupon it became a fashionable interest all over Europe. Systematic excavations began in 1869.

◀ **Left**
Gargoyle fountain at
Schloss Johannisburg

Kaiserpfalz Goslar

In the Middle Ages, Goslar was celebrated as a highly important imperial palace and center of imperial political power. Today the Romanesque Imperial Palace in Goslar is one of the oldest secular buildings in Germany. It is a very rare survivor from over a hundred such palaces, most of which now exist only as ruins.

The reason that Henry II chose Goslar as the site for his palace was the existence of silver, copper and lead mines in Rammelsberg nearby. The emperor moved his palace from Werla to Goslar, choosing a site to the south of the town, at the foot of the mountain where the ore was mined. Henry II renovated and enlarged the palace in the mid-11th century and the most important buildings, the imperial residence and the cathedral, were completed in 1050. Part of the palece was destroyed in a fire in 1065, but it was rebuilt in the same year. During the next century, the Salian monarchs enlarged the palace and built it into a large complex. They added two palace chapels dedicated to St Ulrich and Our Lady, a residential palace and a knights' court. The political role of the Palatinate came to an end when Wilhelm von Holland, the last German emperor to live in Goslar, came to power in 1253. The imperial residence became the property of the town and was altered several times, at one point it was even used as a granary while the chapel became a prison. It was only in 1873 that restoration of the Imperial Palace began. The work took until 1879, and new research has shown that, fundamentally, the reconstruction was carried out correctly.

The largest and most important building of the "most famous palace of the Reich", as chronicler Lampert von Hersfeld described it in his annals, was the Imperial Hall. The two-storied building has a floor area of 164 x 59 ft and is one of the largest existing medieval halls. A projecting porch with two side staircases and a passageway through to the ground floor leads to the first floor, whose facade has six window arcades, each one consisting of three smaller linked arches. A taller arched window in the center with superimposed windows and a gable creates a focal point in the façade, and also indicates that the building houses something special. At this particular point, the Throne Room, the most important room on the first floor, is divided by a transverse section. This is a construction that probably dates from the 12th century and has been a model for many other halls. The wooden beams were only added in 1477 to support the roof, creating a ship-like impression. The hall on the ground floor is lower and has a barrel vault with pointed arches whose vertex is at right angles to the room. An arcaded passage links the hall to the palace chapel of St Ulrich whose facade is decorated with pilaster strips and rounded, arched friezes. It is built on two floors, as was customary in most palaces, so that the servants could attend the services separately from the Emperor and his court. The chapel is built in the shape of an isosceles triangle with a main apse and

RIGHT
The Equestrian statue of Frederick Barbarossa flanks the facade of the Imperial Palace ▶

FOLLOWING DOUBLE SPREAD
A tranquil location. With good reason, Goslar was the favourite palace of Henry III ▶▶

two side apses. In the center is the tomb of the founder, Henry III. Erected in 1884, it contains a reliquary with the Emperor's heart. An open crossing links the ground floor to the octagonal top floor. The apse points eastwards. The frescoes are late Gothic while the chapel itself probably dates from 1100. The Chapel of Our Lady was demolished after falling into disrepair at the end of the 17th century.

Directly in front of the Imperial Palace is the cathedral, of which only the north porch has survived. Indeed, the dilapidated church, consecrated in 1050, was demolished in 1819 because there was no money to restore it. The porch, added in about 1200, was used as a shed by the builders and was therefore spared. The door, with its arcade of round arches, is flanked by double windows. Above the arcade of arches are stucco sculptures, fomerly brightly painted, in wall niches.

The porch is now used to display ancient pieces surviving from the cathedral, such as the highly ornate imperial throne used by the Salian and Hohenstaufen emperors. The throne symbolizes the power of the Goslar Imperial Palatinate in its heyday. The bronze armrests decorated with plant arabesques date from the 11th century, while the stone chair dates from the 12th century when the throne was restored.

The Emperial Palace Goslar now accommodates a museum dedicated to the history of the so-called *Winderkaistertum* (see below).

◄ **LEFT**
Dramatic mural paintings in the St Ulrich chapel of the Imperial Palace of Goslar

The castle church

The "Pfalzen", or imperial palaces, are a German specialty. As early as the mid-13th century, German rulers began to build fixed residences from where they could rule their realms. Until that point the Holy Roman Empire was ruled from royal palaces scattered all over the country. The emperors and kings moved from one palace to another with their courts and furniture, demonstrating by their presence their claim to rule. They held synods and assemblies of the kingdom, dispensed justice as the sole arbiters of right and wrong, and made the vital administrative decisions for the various regions.

Burg Lichtenstein

The slender, elegant silhouette of Burg Lichtenstein rises like a fairytale castle against the skyline, the perfect embodiment of every enchanted castle. It is an imitation of a historic castle, actually built in the 19th century, inspired by the fairytale castles of childhood.

Wilhelm Hauff's historical novel *Lichtenstein* tells the true story of the exiled Duke Ulrich von Württemberg and applies it to the novel's fictional main character Georg von Sturmfeder. This romantic saga of Württemberg history set in the landscape of Swabia made Hauff's novels famous. It also attracted the attention of Duke Wilhelm von Urach, Count of Württemberg, to the ruins of Lichtenstein.

Built in 1390 on a rocky outcrop south of Reutlingen, Lichtenstein castle was believed to be impregnable in the Middle Ages. After it lost its status as a duchy in 1567, it fell into disrepair. The ruins were pulled down in 1802 to make room for a smaller, more modest castle. Duke Wilhelm purchased the ruins of Lichtenstein in 1837 and commissioned Carl Alexander Heideloff to rebuild them. The duke contributed his own ideas and opinions to the plans, strongly influenced by the romantic representations in the novel Lichtenstein.

This resulted in a neo-Gothic historical fantasy incorporating the walls of the old castle up to the second floor. Approached by a narrow little bridge leading to a gateway adorned with battlements and turrets, the main building of the castle consists of a two-story block, joined to another of three stories, both with pointed, arched windows, stepped gables, oriels and pinnacles. Finally there is the slender keep, a tall, elegant tower crowned with battlements. Heideloff's interior of the castle was simply extended around individual older parts such as the Gothic altar and the stained glass windows of the chapel dating from the Middle Ages.

These can therefore be seen in almost their original condition. In the King's Room on the top floor, there is a gallery of ancestral portraits, and the weapons hall is ideal for grand receptions. The present duke lives with his family in the north wing, which is not open to the public.

Right
The novel *Lichtenstein* by Wilhelm Hauff inspired the rebuilding of the ancient ruins in the 19th century as an idealized medieval castle ▶

◀ **Left**
Sculptured figures supporting a bench at Burg Lichtenstein

Feste Marienberg Würzburg

The fortress that dominates the old town of Würzburg is a perfect example of a medieval fortress rebuilt first as a Renaissance castle, and later as a Baroque palace.

The Marienberg fortress was the seat of the prince-bishops of Würzburg until the Residenz Würzburg (see page 78) was built in the 18th century. The oldest buildings, dating back to 706, are in the inner courtyard: the church (Marienkirche), the keep and the pump room that supplied the fortress with water. In 1200, the bishops decided to enlarge the fortress. The royal residence was built and a massive fortress consisting of four walls was constructed round the old buildings. In 1253, Bishop Hermann moved his entire court to the fortress, and from then on the bishops were in a better position to survive their conflicts with the burghers of Würzburg.

Visitors enter the outer, more recent part of the fortress across a drawbridge through the Scherenberg gate, built in 1345 and strengthened in 1482. In about 1600, Prince-Bishop Julius Echter von Mespelbrunn rebuilt the fortress in the Renaissance style. The Echter bastion, named after him and equipped with battlements, was built to reinforce the west side because this was the most vulnerable part of the fortress. (The hill on which it is built is very steep on the other three sides.) The Marienkirche was also rebuilt in Renaissance style. A square chancel in red sandstone was added and the interior decorated with stuccowork. When Feste Marienberg was elevated to the status of a national fortress in 1648, the Baroque fortification walls were added. The two-storied armory was not built until 1711. It is adorned with pillars and displays the coat of arms of Prince-Bishop von Greiffenclau.

The fortress accommodates the Museum für Franken dedicated to the city and cultural history of Würzburg.

Right
Fortress main gate ▶

Following double spread
View of the castle from the Main River ▶▶

◀ **Left**
Corridor leading towards the gateway

Schloss Moritzburg

Schloss Moritzburg is a pleasantly fanciful building with red-tiled towers and a bright yellow facade reflected in the water. This Baroque castle differs from many others because it was originally built in Renaissance times.

The woodlands north of Dresden have always been the hunting grounds of the Saxon electors and kings. It is therefore not surprising that Elector Moritz should have built a hunting lodge there in 1542, named Moritzburg after himself. It was a Renaissance building which was continually enlarged and altered, moving away from the Renaissance towards the Baroque. At the same time, the surrounding woodland was turned into a large hunting park. But it was Elector Frederick Augustus I, better known as Augustus the Strong, who completely rebuilt the castle in the Baroque style. A passionate hunter, he had often used the Moritzburg hunting lodge in his youth and he now wanted to hold court there. To accomplish this he had to modify it so that it would be big enough for large hunting parties and magnificent enough for courtly feasts. The construction work was carried out between 1723 and 1733 under the supervision of Matthäus Daniel Pöppelmann, who was also responsible for the Zwinger in Dresden (see page 114).

The ground plan is unusual with its projecting corner towers that nevertheless form part of an integrated whole. They are linked to the main buildings by narrow connecting wings. The imposing dining hall was designed for Augustus's magnificent banquets and as an architectural counterpart to the castle chapel built on the west side between 1661 and 1672.

The building rests on an almost square, raised terrace measuring 295 x 968 ft as if on a plinth, from which flights of steps with balustrades decorated with carvings lead down to the surrounding island. The castle's awe-inspiring appearance is enhanced by eight little pavilions surrounding it. The lake was created in 1730 after the completion of the castle and fits in very well with the landscape, which already had several smaller ponds. The gardens of the castle island were laid out in the style of French Baroque gardens and extend into the woodland park to the north.

The harmonious interior decoration of Schloss Moritzburg perfectly reflects the serenely beautiful exterior. It is the work of Augustus' interior architect, Raymond Leplat, who always clearly stressed the hunting-lodge character of the castle in his

RIGHT
The walls of the Monströsensaal are decorated with scenes painted by Italian masters ▶

FOLLOWING DOUBLE SPREAD
Masked balls and summer parties were once celebrated in the palace and its magical park ▶▶

◀ **LEFT**
Sculpture detail in the gardens of Schloss Moritzburg

choice of subjects. Fine leather hangings depict scenes relating to the castle and to hunting, such as the "Fishermen's feast on the Moritzburg lake" and scenes from Greek mythology representing Diana, the goddess of hunting. It is these scenes which inspired the name Dianenburg, by which the castle was known during Augustus's lifetime. The hangings are priceless and remarkable both from the point of view of an art historian and for the quality of their craftsmanship. They consist of individual pieces covered with silver leaf and painted with brilliant colors. The tall, white walls of the dining hall continue the hunting theme. They are decorated with deer antlers, while the other rooms contain numerous hunting trophies.

Two main staircases lead from the east and the west to the first floor where the castle chapel, whose decoration is older than that of the rest of the castle, is located. Its walls and ceilings are decorated with white stucco, subtly adorned with gilt, and the altar is particularly magnificent. It was made in 1670 by Johann Fink, who also executed the painted ceiling.

Opposite the main entrance of the castle are the former stables that now house the Saxony stud farm. A parade of stallions takes place during the first three weekends in September.

The castle has a permanent collection and special exhibitions.

Neuschwanstein and Linderhof

Straight out of a dream or a fairytale – Neuschwanstein is the ideal castle. Its superb location, delicate appearance, its magnificent decoration and the legend surrounding King Ludwig II combine to explain the extraordinary fascination of this breathtaking piece of architecture.

Serious art historians believe that this romantic interpretation of the medieval castle goes beyond the limits of good taste. Looking at Neuschwanstein from a purely architectural-historical standpoint, they are probably right. But from a psychological point of view, Neuschwanstein is a blissful, idyllic interpretation of the collective imagination, precisely representing the place everyone envisions at least once as a child. Neuschwanstein can only be properly appreciated and understood when considered in association with its creator King Ludwig II. Ludwig was born the son of Maximilian II on 25 August 1845 in Schloss Nymphenburg (see page 68). He grew up in Schloss Hohenschwangau near Füssen. His strict education and upbringing were bereft of love and affection. His sense of grandeur and his powerful imagination were not encouraged, but, left on his own, he fantasized and imagined himself to be a character in the German mythology that he saw depicted on the walls of Hohenschwangau. He became passionately interested in the works of Schiller and at the age of 16, he saw the

first-ever performance of Richard Wagner's Lohengrin. He identified his romantic ideal in Lohengrin, the knight of the Holy Grail, and became fascinated by all the works of Richard Wagner.

Maximilian II died in 1864 and Louis became king at the age of 18. He threw himself into the business of ruling with great enthusiasm, but he suffered because of differences in opinion with his much older ministers and the pressure of having to agree to wage war against Prussia (1866) and France (1870). But his friendship with Richard Wagner compensated for these pressures. He met the composer soon after ascending to the throne and he supported his artistic ventures. At last Ludwig had found someone who understood and shared his romantic views. In 1868, the king described his plans for Neuschwanstein to Wagner as follows: "I am planning to rebuild the ruins of Hohenschwangau castle near the Pollät gorge in the authentic style of the castles of the German knights of old... The aim is to create one of the most beautiful places pos-

Right
The Bavarian coat of arms supported by ornately carved figures on the central portal at Schloss Linderhof ▶

Following double spread
The well-known fairy tale palace of Neuschwanstein in the breathtaking landscape of the Allgäu was built to imitate an idealized medieval castle ▶▶

◀ Left
Many interiors at Neuschwanstein are decorated with German sagas. The subject in this bedroom is Tristan

sible, holy and unapproachable, a worthy temple for the divine friend who brings about the only salvation and true blessing of the world. You will also find references to Tannhäuser (in the music room with a view of the castle in the background) and Lohengrin (in the bailey, the open passage and the route to the chapel). This castle will be more beautiful and more homely than Hohenschwangau castle below, which is desecrated every year by my mother's prose. The desecrated gods will take revenge and come and live with us high above the steep rock, surrounded by the heavenly air." Construction of the castle began in 1869 and Ludwig devoted an increasing amount of time to it, while the problems of governing his kingdom also grew. Building continued for 17 years and was never really completed. The king paid for the construction of Neuschwanstein from his private fortune, as he had done for the other castles, Linderhof nearby and Herrenchiemsee on an island in the Chiemsee. However, in 1886 he had debts of 13 million marks with an income of only 5.5 million marks. Neuschwanstein is not just a deliberate copy of a medieval knight's castle – Wartburg (see page 96) was the original inspiration – but an idealized new creation. Significantly, the castle was not designed by an architect, but by a stage set designer and scene painter, Christian Jank. Bay windows, turrets, columns and arcades adorn the five-storied palace and give it an airy, light appearance. This impression is enhanced by the castle's spectacular location on a rocky outcrop 3,300 ft high, overlooking the Alps and the waters of Schwansee. The lavish interior decoration was inspired by German mythology and Wagner's works. Thus, the dressing room is adorned with motifs from the life of Walther von der Vogelweide, a medieval ballad singer. The theme in the bedroom, decorated in neo-Gothic style, depicts scenes from the story of Tristan. The Tannhäuser saga is told in an imposing wall painting by Joseph Aigner in the study.

The throne room is decorated with Byzantine wall paintings depicting Christ, the twelve apostles and the kings of Christendom. This sumptuous throne room, reminiscent of a chapel, symbolizes an idealized "glorious kingdom", which Ludwig was unfortunately unable to replicate in his own country. Whether or not he would have been able to achieve it if he had devoted more time to affairs of state is debatable. Ludwig's political opponents hatched a plot against him and had him declared insane, using his enormous expenditure on building as evidence. Proof of insanity was the only means to depose a king. No one dared to examine him personally, but a respected psychiatrist, Dr Gudden, agreed to write a medical report based solely on witness statements and files without ever having met the king. On 10 June 1886, a number of highly placed people went to Neuschwanstein to depose the king. However, the king had been warned and had the group arrested. He released them the same evening. On the night of the June 11, Ludwig was overpowered in the south tower and taken to Schloss Berg on Starnbergersee. The following day, the king and Dr Gudden went for a walk from which neither returned. They were both found drowned in the lake. The exact circumstances were never clarified. Did the king commit suicide or was he murdered?

In 2007, seven new wonders of the world were selected, Neuschwanstein ended up 8th.

◀ **LEFT**
The grotto at Neuschwanstein recalls Lohengrin's boat pulled by a swan

FOLLOWING DOUBLE SPREAD
The royal villa at Linderhof was often used as a private refuge by the reclusive King Ludwig ▶▶

Schloss Nymphenburg

Designed as a summer residence for the wife of the Elector of Bavaria, this little Italian-style building developed into one of the most imposing Baroque palaces in Europe.

Elector Ferdinand Maria of Bavaria (1636-79) presented the Kemnat region near Munich as a gift to his wife Henriette Adelaide of Savoy on the birth of their son, the heir to the throne. In 1664 the Electress asked the Italian architect Agostino Barelli to build her a summer residence in the style of a Roman villa. This original summer residence became the central part of Nymphenburg. In 1701, Henriette's son Maximilian Emmanuel, now regent, commissioned Enrico Zuccali to enlarge the summer villa with the addition of side galleries and residential pavilions. Interrupted by the War of the Spanish Succession, the development of the palace was taken over by Joseph Effner in 1714. He built the wings at right angles to each end of the existing building, making a large courtyard, and modernized the original facade of the central building in the French style. The modest summer residence thus became a Baroque palace widely praised by the people of the time.

Under Elector Karl Albrecht (1697-1745), Henriette's grandson who later became Emperor Charles VII, Nymphenburg was further enlarged by additions in the Rococo style. Between 1729 and 1758, curved buildings were built to from a semicircle closing off the courtyard and marking the boundary between the vast castle complex and the city of Munich.

The gardens also developed over the years, becoming ever larger and more beautiful with time. In the mid-18th century, Ludwig von Sckell converted the Baroque

park into a beautiful classical landscaped garden. The central axes of the parterres and central canal with its cascade were preserved, but the other regular geometric axes and avenues were replaced by natural features. This successful combination of two fundamentally different gardening styles gives the park a particular fascination while its basic structure has remained the same.

Plenty of time is required to visit the Nymphenburg palace and park and enjoy its many delights. There are also several museums, several smaller Rococo pavilions in the park, the botanical gardens, and the Palm café in the park to provide a welcome break.

The visit starts in the two story Great Hall designed by Johann Baptist Zimmermann in exuberant Rococo style with ornate ceiling paintings depicting the gods, including the goddess Flora surrounded by nymphs paying tribute to her. The central hall divides the building in two halves, one housing the apartments of the Electress and the other those of the

RIGHT
The luxuriantly rococo Hall of Mirrors in the Amalienburg, one of the pavilions in the park ▶

FOLLOWING DOUBLE SPREAD
The original summer villa, symmetrically flanked by the residential pavilions, is set in the formal baroque landscaping of the park ▶▶

◀ **LEFT**
A fabulous gilded carriage in the Museum of Royal Carriages

Elector. Each apartment consists of four rooms, some of which still have the original Baroque painted ceilings.

The left wing of the castle now houses the Museum of Royal Carriages, which has many exhibits associated with the transport of the sovereign family, including carriages, coaches, sleighs and harnesses. In the Museum of Nymphenburg Porcelain, exquisite examples of work from this factory can be admired. The opposite wing houses the Museum Mensch und Natur, the natural science museum, where the development of the earth with its flora and fauna is explained in a modern, child-friendly way using multimedia aids.

There are four small pavilions in the park, of which the Amalienburg with its rotundas and two side wings is the most elegant. François de Cuvilliés built it between 1734 and 1739 as a hunting lodge for the Electress Amalie who asked for a raised hide to be built on the domed roof. Reflecting the pavilion's function, the interior decor depicts hunting subjects and compositions including the goddess Diana, the huntress. The Hall of Mirrors is not to be missed, decorated in blue and silver with stuccowork by Zimmerman and carvings by Joachim Dietrich, all executed in the finest Rococo.

The Badenburg, built 1718–21, served a completely different purpose. Max Emanuel commissioned Joseph Effner to build him a lodge for bathing. The Badenburg has a heated indoor swimming pool for bathing with a visitors' gallery on the upper floor. The Pagodenburg, built in the French style in 1716-19 on the lake of the same name, is furnished in the Chinese style with silk rugs and lacquer work. The Magdalenenklause (Magdalena Hermitage) is quite different from the other three buildings. It is behind the palm house, slightly concealed by greenery, and was designed as a hermit's cell, a secluded place for reflection.

The botanical garden in the north section of the park was moved here from Karlsplatz in 1914. It includes about 150 varieties of rhododendrons that flower in May and June. Munich's botanical garden is one of the most important in Europe with some 6,000 types of plants growing in the garden's greenhouses.

Nymphenburg porcelain

The Nymphenburg porcelain factory was founded in 1747 and has been located at Schloss Nymphenburg since 1761. Nymphenburg porcelain can be identified by its distinctive Bavarian diamond mark, which dates from 1754. It is famous for its figures of the Commedia dell'Arte, designed by Anton Bustelli. The factory can be visited by appointment only and applications must be made in writing.

WASSERSCHLOSS RAESFELD

"Here, high up in the stone gallery, surmounted by a slate-covered cupola with a small chiming mechanism, the wind blows round the tower and over the land; below is the moat covered with water-lilies and pondweed, the sleepy, pointed, red roofs of the laborers' houses and the peaceful chapel, flanked by two towers..." This description of Schloss Raesfeld is from Gustav Sack's novel "Ein verbummelter Student" ("An idle student") published in 1918.

The Münsterland, with its flat fields and meadows, is home to hundreds of castles, all with one particular feature in common – a moat. Regardless of whether the building in question is a small manor house type of residence or a much larger edifice, the castles are all surrounded by a broad stretch of water designed to keep intruders and attackers at bay. Many moated castles are still in an excellent state of preservation, partly because they continued to serve as the seat of local noble families and provided a good base for administering the surrounding estates.

Wasserschloss Raesfeld is situated west of Münster – one of the towns that formed part of the Treaty of Westphalia – close to the Dutch border. Its distinctive architectural style and unusual corner tower bear testimony to the two main builders' determination to leave their mark on the castle, although only two of the original four wings have survived.

The north wing, with its ground floor, two main floors and a top story is an essentially 15th-century construction. After a fire at the beginning of the 17th century, Alexander I von Vehlen had it rebuilt in the Renaissance style. He also added a somewhat smaller, round tower to the northern corner of the extremely imposing, tiled and gabled house.

Having inherited considerable property and a sound financial cushion from his father, Alexander II – a favorite of the Kaiser during the Thirty Years' War – went on to amass even greater wealth. In 1643 he used this money to extend Burg Raesfeld into a residence befitting his personal standing.

Michael of Ghent built the west wing and five-story tower. This tower, which looks a little like a secularized church tower, is topped by an unusual cupola: the upper part appears to consist of three sections stacked one on top of the other, rising very steeply and ending in an onion-shaped dome. This unique design does not belong to any particular architectural style, yet it has become a symbol of the Münsterland region. Complementing it at the other end of the long main section, at the front of the castle, is a somewhat smaller tower. Alexander II had an observatory constructed in the lantern at the top of this structure.

The castle nowadays accommodates an institute for advanced studies.

RIGHT
The typical moated castle of Raesfeld is now the home of a crafts organization ▶

FOLLOWING DOUBLE SPREAD
To provide protection from enemies, the building was constructed within an impassable defensive moat ▶▶

Residenz, Würzburg

The Residenz of Würzburg can be accurately described as a European rather than a German castle. Probably the most ambitious building project of 18th century Germany, it involved some of the most distinguished masters of European architecture. The result is a perfect synthesis of European Baroque.

The prince-bishops of Würzburg had lived in Feste Marienberg (see page 52) since 1250. During the 18th century, they decided to build a more accessible palace in the city, as a lasting and imposing monument to the glory of the House of Schönborn and its loyalty to the Emperor. In 1720, Prince-Bishop Johann Philipp von Schönborn laid the foundation stone of the Würzburg Residenz. The whole family was interested in the project and contributed with suggestions. Famous architects and designers from all over Europe were employed, and advice was sought from Johann Lukas von Hildebrandt from Vienna, architect of Schloss Belvedere (see page 120), Robert de Cotte and Germain Boffrand of Paris. Johann Wolfgang von der Auvera and Antonio Bossi were commissioned as sculptors and carvers to create the interior stucco decoration, and the celebrated Venetian artist Giovanni Battista Tiepolo was commissioned to decorate the staircase and the Kaisersaal (imperial room) with magnificent frescoes. This explains the French, Italian, Flemish and Austrian influences. The most important individual was Balthasar Neumann, the main architect, responsible for the basic plans, for coordinating the construction of the Residenz and combining all these influences into a brilliant expression of Baroque design. Neumann is sometimes described as the project's "secret" architect because he supervised the construction from beginning to end, and survived three successive prince-bishops.

The rectangular ground plan is that of a typical French Baroque palace: a long, narrow central part with two side-wings at right angles to it, an aspect that associates it with the Italian "urban villa". Typically, the inner courtyards are formed by these side wings. There is a raised ground floor and a main floor, each with a mezzanine floor above it. These mezzanine floors lighten the appearance of the facade and also provided space for servants' accommodation. The exterior facades are very ornate but not excessively so because of the classical regularity introduced by the windows and pilasters. The west entrance facade is embellished with a projecting porch overlooking the main courtyard.

RIGHT
Balthasar Neumann designed this wonderful staircase while Tiepolo painted the largest ceiling painting in the world above it ▶

FOLLOWING DOUBLE SPREAD
The formal gardens in front of the Residenz are rococo style, filled with flower beds, topiaries, trellises and arcades ▶▶

◀ **LEFT**
Ingeniously designed promenades lead the visitor through the spectacular gardens

This facade has no mezzanine floor, but instead has a balcony that runs above the three arcade-like entrances. Three French windows lead from the White Room onto this balcony. The roof line is ornamented with balustrades and interrupted above the porch by a curved front gable displaying the coat of arms of the last patron, Friedrich Carl von Schönborn, who completed the construction in 1774.

This porch leads into the hall adjacent to the Gartensaal or garden room on the ground floor to the east. The high vaulted ceiling is supported by slender marble columns that give it the appearance of floating, while at the same time forming lateral arches that form a side ambulatory passage round the room. Johann Zick's ceiling frescoes depict subjects related to the garden: the "Rest of Diana" and a "Sumptuous meal". The stuccowork is by Bossi and emphasizes the overall impression of the lightness of this room.

The hall also leads to the staircase, which epitomizes the status to which its owners aspired. Tiepolo gave free rein to his vivid imagination, taking visitors by surprise with his imagery. The ceiling fresco only develops fully from the second flight of stairs onward. The vaulted ceiling is 105 ft long, 59 ft wide and 16 ft deep. It is an incredible architectural achievement, because it lacks visible support. The large area was lavishly decorated by Tiepolo in grandiose style. One of the largest frescoes in the world, its southern part includes an exalted portrait of the prince-bishop, in which Mercury is seen fleeing from Olympus. Allegories of the four continents (Australia was not discovered until 1777) are depicted at the sides, and directly above the entrance to the White Room is Europa, surrounded by artists. Tiepolo himself can be seen in the corner on the left and Neumann reclines in the center. The Weissersaal (white room) is entirely decorated in matte white, without any color or gold decoration, creating an area of tranquility between the sumptuousness of the staircase and the Kaisersaal. Bossi's grandiose stucco sculptures are unique in their refinement and elegance and are one of the high points of Rococo decoration.

The top floor of the central building contains the Kaisersaal – the most impressive and sumptuous room of the Würzburg Residenz, where indeed several emperors have been officially received. Tiepolo's frescoes decorating the cupola depict a "bridal procession" with Apollo carrying the bride in his sun chariot to the emperor. Tiepolo has also depicted scenes from the history of Würzburg with Frederick Barbarossa in the center. The paintings above the doors are by Tiepolo's son Domenico. The only parts of the room not decorated with stucco by Bossi and frescoes by Tiepolo are the walls, which are covered with stucco marble.

Leading from the Kaisersaal in both directions are the north and south imperial apartments, about 500 ft long. These are sumptuous rooms with magnificent carved doorframes and window frames. The castle chapel in the west part of the south wing does not stand out from the rest of the building, but is completely integrated within the structure of the palace. There is a dramatic surprise on entering, because its height spans two floors. The Baroque interior with its three cupolas is spectacular.

◀ **LEFT**
Monumental Fountain at the Residenz of Würzburg

Burg Rheinfels and Burg Katz

For centuries the beauty of the Rhine has been celebrated and visited by countless admirers, especially its most famous stretch, the German middle Rhine. Its picturesque landscape still attracts large numbers of visitors today, as do the numerous castles along its bank. The stretch near St Goar is particularly appealing with the castles of Burg Rheinfels and Burg Katz, as well as the famous Lorelei rock.

Burg Rheinfels was known as the "Guard on the Rhine" until the 18th century when the French destroyed the outworks. A year later, they also destroyed the keep and the fortress itself – a sad end for probably the most powerful fortress of the middle Rhine. It was originally constructed in 1245 by Count Diether V von Katzenelnbogen who built a hilltop fortress with a square ground plan and keep on a rocky outcrop along the Rhine. It demonstrated its impregnability just eleven years later when it successfully resisted a siege by the League of Rhenish towns, after which it was believed to be invincible. But it was captured several times in the following centuries in spite of its strengthened fortifications.

In the 14th century, Count Wilhelm II (who also built Burg Katz fortress on the other bank of the Rhine in 1371) increased the height of the keep of Burg Rheinfels and built new living quarters. The ancient moat was further secured by a high wall on the mountainside, with a tower at each end. Modern arms technology in the 16th century led to the building of outworks and casemates along the Rhine and the south side. The moat was roofed over so that the castle courtyard could be enlarged and a cellar was created. The building was also extended by the addition of half-timbered buildings to become a comfortable residence for Prince Philipp II von Hessen-Rheinfels. In the 17th century, the military structures of the fortress were further improved by the addition of mine passages in the southwest. Later, the "Noli me tangere" fortification and the Scharfeneck fort were added. Nevertheless the French finally succeeded in capturing Burg Rheinfels and destroyed much of it forever in 1796-97. Today only about one-third of the original structure survives, but it has not lost its imposing appearance. In 2017, a start was made with a comprehensive renovation of the castle, during which the castle will remain

Right:
Castle Katz rises on a mountain spur above St Goarshausen ▶

Following double spread
Schloss Rhinefels, once one of the mightiest defence installations of the middle Rhine ▶▶

◀ **Left**
Statue of the Lorelei at the Lorelei rock

open to visitors. Opposite Berg Rheinfels on the other side of the Rhine is Neu-Katzeneln-nbogen, or Berg Katz, built by Wilhelm II on the same plan as Berg Rheinfels. It suffered the same fate as its imposing elder sister and was destroyed by the French in 1806. It had never been as strongly fortified as its neighbor opposite because of its location on the other side of the river. It was rebuilt between 1896 and 1898, when the Romantic period was at its height in Germany. Only the keep was left as a ruin.

Berg Katz overlooks one of Germany's most famous landmarks, the Lorelei. The legendary rock, made famous by Heinrich Heine's poem, "Die Lorelei", overlooks a narrow pass on the Rhine. At this point, the river is just 367 ft wide, only about one-third of its usual width, and dominated by the Lorelei rock towering 433 ft above the water. In the past, many ships went aground at this dangerous spot.

It was the German romantic poet, Clemens Brentano, who "personified" this rock, turning its ancient name, "Lurley," ("Lei" or "Ley" means "stone") into a woman's name. He invented the siren Lore Ley and introduced her in 1801 in his novel Godwi. Through no fault of her own, the wonderfully beautiful girl with blond hair became the undoing of many sailors because they no longer watched the dangerous waters, but only had eyes for Lore Ley. She threw herself into the Rhine and drowned to escape the unwanted power with which she was cursed. Heine used the story in his popular poem, which became still more famous later when Frederick Silcher set it to music. The fortress is privately owned and unfortunately not open to the public.

SCHLOSS SANSSOUCI

Tired of fighting after five years of the Silesian Wars, Frederick the Great said "Let us live and enjoy life". Accordingly, he built a pleasure palace in Potsdam, southwest of Berlin where he could spend the summer "free from care" – "sans souci" in French – pursuing his musical and philosophical interests with his friends. The result was the Palace of Sansouci and its gardens, representing a complete synthesis of German Rococo.

Frederick II (1712–1786) commissioned the architect Georg Wenzeslaus von Knobelsdorff to build him his pleasure palace. The long, semi-circular main building was based on the French maisons de plaisance or "pleasure houses", and it was built among the terraced vineyards of Potsdam between 1745 and 1747. More buildings were added until 1770, including the Neue Palais and Belvedere. Frederick William IV (1795–1861) enlarged Sanssouci further with landscaped gardens, Roman baths, a pheasantry and the Friedenskirche church.

There are justly celebrated views from the palace of the large fountains in the park across six terraces planted with vines and of the wide flight of steps leading towards the copper cupola. Large windows and doors, framed by statues of bacchanals made by the sculptor Frederick Christian Glume and the golden-yellow facade give the rather compact building charm and grace. The structure of the garden front reflects the terraced vineyards so that the castle looks like the crowning conclusion of the landscape.

The main entrance is on the far side of the building, where colonnades of Corinthian columns on both sides of the palace enclose the main courtyard, forming a quadrant. There are only twelve rooms in the main building of Sanssouci, each of them decorated by von Knobelsdorff in the finest Rococo style. It is easy to imagine Frederick's guests driving through the main courtyard in their carriages dazzled by the impressive entrance hall of the main building, decorated with exuberant Rococo ornamentation of gilded stucco, marble and ceiling paintings. If the guests were members of Frederick's famous "Round tables", they would be taken to the elegant marble hall. In the elegant room of white marble decorated with gilt, this enlightened philosopher-king met with intellectuals from all over the world, including the French writer and satirist Voltaire.

When the monarch was not busy debating and philosophizing, he spent his time in his beautiful library, lined with cedar wood paneling, writing poetry; or

RIGHT
The superb library with cedar wood panelling and rococo gilt ormulu ▶

FOLLOWING DOUBLE SPREAD
View of the summer palace, Sanssouci, from the south-east terrace. Here the philosopher Frederick would wander in deep thought ▶▶

◀ **LEFT**
Statue of the goddess Minerva/Athena

he would compose music or play the flute in the music room, probably the most beautiful room in Sanssouci. It is in this magnificent Rococo room, with its striking white and gold decor, that he gave some of the chamber concerts immortalized by Adolph Menzel in his painting, "Flute concert at Sanssouci". The large mirrors in the room create an enchanting atmosphere, because while making it look larger, they also appear to bring the greenery of the gardens into the room.

The gardens were originally designed in Rococo style by von Knobelsdorff with neat flower-beds, formal pools of water, geometrically planned paths and visual axes. In 1816, they were redesigned in the style of the English landscape gardens where everything was planted and laid out with great care to produce a natural effect. The gardens were redesigned by the famous Prussian garden designer, Peter Joseph Lenné.

Several other buildings were built in the park, such as the Drachenhaus (Dragon House) and the Klausberg Belvedere. Destroyed by a bomb in World War II, only the ruins remain of this elliptical pavilion (which originally consisted of two superimposed columned halls), but the view from it of the park and the surrounding Havelland countryside is still breathtaking. The Dragon House on the southern slope was built in the 18th century in the style of a three-tiered Chinese pagoda with dragons on each corner of the roof. Today it is used as a coffee-house in the summer.

The Chinese teahouse, a high point of Frederick the Great's Rococo, was inspired by a passion for all things oriental. He personally designed this pavilion and Gottfried Bühring built it between 1754 and 1757. It has a tent-like roof supported by gilt palm trees and a cupola surmounted by a golden mandarin with a Chinese sunshade. Everywhere there are paintings, sculptures and stuccos depicting oriental themes.

To the west, the imposing Neue Palais (New Palace), built at the end of the main visual axis, marks the boundary of the park. Frederick the Great built it between 1763 and 1769 as a symbol of Prussian power, with 400 rooms distributed over three floors. A total of 230 pilasters and 428 statues and sculptures adorn the facade of the main building, which is dominated by a mighty cupola resting on a cylindrical base. Across from it are the offices and outbuildings, built in the same style as the Palais itself with flights of stairs and cupolas, thus giving them the appearance of little chateaus.

The Rococo style of the exterior of the Neue Palais is reflected in the interior: the magnificent marble gallery and the grotto hall adorned with semi-precious stones and fossils. The addition of niches decorated with glass and coral fragments contributes further to the grotto atmosphere.

The marble gallery is very striking with its red jasper and white Carrara marble walls and floor. Both the marble gallery and the grotto were designed by Carl von Gontard. In the south wing of the Neue Palais is a theater that was only used on very special occasions.

◀ **LEFT**
The Chinese tea house is an expression of the 18th century taste for the oriental

FOLLOWING DOUBLE SPREAD
Interior view of the picture gallery, the oldest museum building in Germany, with its display of works by European masters ▶▶

WARTBURG, EISENACH

No other castle has become such a monument to German history as the Wartburg castle. It is true that its name is usually associated with Martin Luther who once lived there, but the legendary choral contests of ballad singers and the Wartburg festival of German students are events that have become inseparably associated with it.

The building of the Wartburg castle on top of a hill near present-day Eisenach was first mentioned in historical documents in 1080. Ludwig der Springer ("Louis the Knight") wanted to ensure and expand the power of the Ludowingers and he soon realized that this fortress was an ideal strategic point of departure for colonizing the surrounding Thuringian region. Over a century later, in 1131, the Ludowingers were made landgraves and Wartburg became their residence. In 1172, Ludwig III felt the time had come to express his new power and status architecturally, by surrounding himself with a more magnificent court. He built a three-storied Romanesque palace, and the central part of the complex is still considered a masterpiece of traditional castle architecture today.

There is a passageway behind the arcades, while the top floor houses a vast banqueting hall that can accommodate several hundred people. It is possible, although not historically documented, that the famous contest of ballad singers was first held in this hall in about 1206. In 1190, during the reign of Landgrave Hermann I, Wartburg became the intellectual and cultural center of the Middle Ages. In 1203, the Middle High German poet Wolfram von Eschenbach lived at the Wartburg court, and Walther von der Vogelweide extolled Hermann I's patronage of intellectual life in his poetry. Hermann I is believed to have organized the first singing competition at Wartburg. This became known as the contest of ballad singers and was incorporated by Richard Wagner in his opera "Tannhäuser". It is quite possible that this

event really did take place, because similar troubadour traditions at Swabian and Austrian courts have been historically documented. The magnificent fresco created by Moritz von Schwind in 1854–55 depicts how such a contest of ballad singers might have looked.

What is unequivocally certain is the fact that Martin Luther stayed at Wartburg. He took refuge there on 4 May 1521 after being declared an outlaw by the Reichstag of Worms. He stayed several months at Wartburg using the pseudonym "Junker Jörg". During this time, he wrote pamphlets and books on the

◀ **LEFT**
View of the inner
courtyard. The Vogtei
with its famous Luther
room is on the left side

reformation and translated the New Testament into German, thus laying the foundation for the Reformation. Luther introduced the interpretation of Christianity based on the Bible, making it the focus of the church whose shortcomings it was supposed to overcome. This criticism of the papacy and Catholic dogma finally led to the schism between the Catholics and Protestants. Lucas Cranach the Elder painted this influential religious personality in his "Portrait of Martin Luther as Junker Jörg". This portrait is on display at Wartburg, together with other exhibits such as first editions of Luther's writings and Reformation pamphlets.

On 18 and 19 October 1817, some 500 students came to Wartburg to celebrate the 300th anniversary of the Reformation and the fourth anniversary of the Battle of the Nations, fought near Leipzig in 1813. The Students' duelling society burned the Act of the German Confederation and demanded a united Germany with a constitution. This Wartburg festival became a political and liberal demonstration against reactionaries and an early manifestation of German nationalism.

Johann von Goethe was dismissive of these hotheaded students, but nevertheless the great German poet (who often stayed at Wartburg) prompted the Weimar Grand Duke to renovate the dilapidated Wartburg castle as a symbol of the German nation. The restoration eventually started in 1838 under Carl Alexander, and was less a reconstruction of the medieval fortress than the realization of a romantic idea of Wartburg as a court of chivalry, as it was imagined in the 19th century.

The fortress was enlarged by the addition of a keep, a gate tower and other constructions. The interior decoration, complete with magnificent frescoes painted by Moritz von Schwind, had very little in common with the harsh reality of medieval life. But the extent to which Wartburg reflected the ideas of the people at the time is shown by the reaction of Ludwig II after visiting the castle in 1867. "This dream that has materialized into stone," he said, and it certainly inspired him when building Schloss Neuschwanstein (see page 60).

The most recent restoration work since the 1950s took the medieval past of the fortress into account as well as changes in valuing the past. Indeed, the castle's history of almost 1,000 years means that it includes remains of various periods, and those dating from the 19th century are now as important as earlier ones because they represent a particular period of history just as much as the parts dating from the Middle Ages. The plainness of the Lutheran era is reflected in Luther's room and the Reformation room. The ground floor of the palace conveys the romantic atmosphere of the Middle Ages, while the banqueting hall on the top floor reflects the splendor of Germany's glory years (1871–73). All these different styles illustrate how much Wartburg is bound to the history of Germany.

Wartburg was the first German castle added to the UNESCO World Heritage list in 1999.

Wilhelmshöhe, Kassel

The imposing statue of Hercules that stands on the wooded mountain top in the gardens of Wilhelmshöhe appears like an enormous guide pointing the way to the classical castle. Hercules, the highest point in Kassel, has become the symbol of the largest city in north Hesse.

The three mile long Wilhelmshöhe entrance drive runs dead straight from the two guard lodges of Oberneustadt to the castle and beyond, in a visual axis to the statue of Hercules on the eastern edge of the Habicht forest. Thus it links the city not only to the castle, but also to the surrounding woods. The copper statue of Hercules, created by Johann Jacob Anthoni in 1717, symbolizes nature conquered by man, a theme that is repeated everywhere in the gardens. The statue is nearly 30 ft tall and stands at the top of a stone pyramid 98 ft high, which in turn crowns a giant octagonal structure. A water cascade 500 ft long and over 33 ft wide rushes from a basin at the base of this octagon. The basin is 93 ft high, and mounted on steps divided into three sections. It is an unusual idea executed on a remarkable scale, and with it the Landgrave Karl certainly built himself a unique monument.

Pursuing the symbolism of the Hercules monument, Karl laid out completely geometric formal Baroque gardens, of which little has survived. In the second half of the 18th century, Landgrave Frederick II and Elector Wilhelm I turned the gardens into a wonderful landscaped park with soft, flowing outlines, manmade streams, meadows and specially planted groups of trees, imitating and competing with nature. Nothing was overlooked or left to chance. Many rare species of trees were planted and the example of traditional English landscaped gardens was carefully copied. Many follies were built, such as the ruins of a Roman aqueduct, a Virgilian monument, a Sybilline grotto, a temple of Mercury and a devil's bridge.

Between 1786 and 1798, Elector Wilhelm I commissioned the architect Simon Louis du Ry to rebuild the castle completely in classical style, thus entirely replacing the Renaissance building. The rebuilding was carried out in stages. First the white stone building to the south was erected, followed by the church wing to the north. Both buildings have a central projection with imposing rows of columns reaching up to the top floor and an upper story whose balustrade is decorated with urns. The next

RIGHT
Part of the baroque park with the devil's bridge ▶

FOLLOWING DOUBLE SPREAD
Inspired by English medieval castles, the Löwenburg (Lion castle) was designed as an intimate refuge for Elector Wilhelm IX ▶▶

◀ **LEFT**
The focal point of Wilhemshöhe was the copper statue of Hercules, a landmark for the city of Kassel

stage involved the construction of the central building with a six-column portico and triangular pediment, surmounted by a cupola which was destroyed in World War II and never rebuilt. The two rounded, slightly lower wings (that link the central building with the two lateral wings) were erected in 1829. The courtyard in front of the long, curved building overlooks the mountain and the eye follows the park across the cascade to the statue of Hercules. In 1822, the large greenhouse was built. It is a magical place, full of wonderful plants and especially welcoming on rainy days. This greenhouse is typical of 19th century industrial architecture and is one of Germany's oldest cast iron and glass constructions.

The Staatliche Gemäldegalerie (public picture gallery) has one of the largest collections of Old Masters in Germany after Munich, Dresden and Berlin. It includes works by Rembrandt, Dürer, Rubens and van Dyck. The museum also has a collection of classical Greek and Roman antiquities, of which the Kassel Apollo is the most famous exhibit.

Only the white stone wing still has its period furnishings and furniture, an indication of the rapid changes in aristocratic interior design between 1760 and 1830. Some of the pieces are still the original Louis XVI furniture while the others are English, a style much favored by the royal house of Hesse from the second half of the 18th century onwards. However, the furniture also includes Empire style pieces dating from the period of Jérôme Bonaparte and the restoration after 1815. Particularly impressive is the bathroom with wood-paneled walls, a marble bath sunk in the floor, a Venetian chandelier, a sofa and armchairs.

The Löwenburg

In the late 18th century, the whole of Germany was possessed by a passion for romantic ruins, and Elector Wilhelm had an artificial half-ruined castle constructed in a hidden corner of the park. Known as the Löwenburg (Lion castle), this was his intimate refuge, a place where he could withdraw for undisturbed moments, alone or with his mistresses. The architect Johann Christoph Wussow was engaged by the prince to translate his lyrical ideas into reality and from 1793 to 1806 he created a medieval castle that was to some extent inspired by English examples. He grouped the buildings round a rectangular courtyard and equipped it with everything that in the 18th century was identified as part of a "genuine" castle: a mott and bailey, battlements and rampart walks, moats and drawbridges. Everything that today is seen in a picturesque state of decay was originally built in this state. The Löwenburg was a famous and influential curiosity and after seeing it many nobles bought old castle ruins to restore. In the apse of the castle chapel lies the monument of Elector Wilhelm I, who was buried here in fulfillment of his wishes.

◀ **LEFT**
These parts of the Löwenburg reveal the extraordinary romantic enthusiasm for the Middle Ages. They were designed as ruins from the start

Schloss Wörlitz

Built at the end of the 18th century, Schloss Wörlitz is quite unlike Germany's old castles that have been expanded and altered throughout the centuries. It is more of a country house, a well-planned building based on an overall concept – to be precise, the concept of civic enlightenment. It was on the basis of these principles that the first large-scale landscaped park was created on the European continent, and the foundations of neo-classical and Gothic revival architecture in Germany were laid.

Prince Leopold III Frederick Francis von Anhalt-Dessau (1740–1817) was motivated by civic enlightenment, the spiritual movement of the 17th and 18th centuries which rejected the authority of the church and the absolute state, subjected traditional standards and institutions to critical examination and believed that human understanding was the only way to assess truth and morality. This concept is clearly illustrated at Wörlitz, which was influenced by the prince's travels through England and Italy. He turned his small principality – and thus his residence in Wörlitz – into a center of interest for enlightened intellectuals. Johann Wolfgang von Goethe, Alexander von Humboldt, Jean-Jacques Rousseau and Joachim Winckelmann are just a few of the great intellectual geniuses who exchanged ideas in Schloss Wörlitz.

The English-style park, with gardens, landscaped expanses, canals, islands and buildings, including the little castle, stretches across 250 acres around Lake Wörlitz between the Elbe to the north, with its numerous meadows, and the village of Wörlitz to the west, with its 2,000 inhabitants. It is situated in green surroundings south of the lake, a short distance from the village. The brick castle was designed by Frederick Wilhelm von Erdmannsdorff (1736–1800) who was a close friend, counselor and travel companion of the prince. Building began in 1769 and continued until 1773.

It was built in the style of an English country house, inspired by the work of the Italian architect Andrea Palladio. Wörlitz, with its portico supported by four Corinthian columns and its sober main façade, was clearly inspired by Claremont in Surrey, not far from London. The lakeside facade is even more functional and reflects the influence of classical Greek and Roman architecture, as a contrast to the Baroque style associated with absolute monarchy. In fact, the prince, who was affectionately yet respectfully known as

RIGHT
Schloss Wörtlitz was built in the style of an English country house ▶

FOLLOWING DOUBLE SPREAD
Like a typical English country house, the main front has a central portico with Corinthian columns ▶▶

◀ **LEFT**
White bridge in the Schloss Wörlitz gardens

"Father Franz" by his subjects, turned the ground floor into a museum, accessible to the public, while he and his wife lived on the top floor.

The interior decoration by Erdmannsdorff has largely been preserved, and clearly illustrates how much the castle forms a unified whole. Everything is well-structured and the classical influence was not ignored here either, especially in the stucco and grisaille paintings on the ceilings and walls. The library is a real gem with its bookcases, frescoes and busts of famous literary figures and scholars.

The Gothic house on the other side of the lake was also designed by Erdmannsdorff, and built between 1773 and 1813. It is quite apparent that the house was inspired by an Italian church, Santa Maria dell'Orto. The facade overlooking the park is divided into three parts by white supporting pillars, cornices and architraves. This part of the building was erected in 1773–74 while the rest was only built ten years later, the style reflecting the various phases of English Gothic. The last part of the building was finally erected in 1811 to house the collections of 16th and 17th century Swiss glass which can still be seen today.

In Franz's time, cows used to graze in the pastures in front of the Gothic House, making clear to the visitors that the prince took the principles of enlightenment seriously. This was also reflected in the park, which was landscaped but took natural conditions and the needs of people into account. There were areas specifically designated for cattle, fruit and vines. The prince did not feel above such "banal" uses of his park, and he was personally involved even in the culture of silkworms. The layout of the gardens, designed by Prince Franz and his friend Erdmannsdorff, had already begun in 1764, before the castle was built, and spanned four years. The Neumark garden with its labyrinth of rocky paths symbolizing the tortuous path of human life was created in the southwest part of the park; in the middle of the labyrinth stood the busts of two German Enlightenment philosophers – Christian Fürchtegott Gellert and Johann Kaspar Lavater. Like the castle, the park was open to the public. Goethe's impressions of the gardens, which he described to Baroness von Stein in a letter in 1778, are still confirmed by visitors today. "It is incredibly beautiful, I was very moved yesterday as I wandered among lakes, canals and little woods, and realized how the gods had made it possible for the prince to create this dream world. Strolling through it is like entering a fairytale that is being told to one, reminiscent of the Elysian Fields where gentle diversity flows to become one. There is nothing to attract one to a particular point; one goes round without ever wondering where one started and where one is going."

ZWINGER, DRESDEN

The Zwinger, situated in the center of Dresden, is one of the most beautiful Baroque monuments. It is not its size that impresses – the Zwinger is relatively small – but the harmonious unity of the architecture and its sculptural details is particularly pleasing.

Elector Frederick Augustus I, known as Augustus der Starke or Augustus the Strong was a typical Baroque prince, art enthusiast and generous patron. Furthermore, he had a large court for which he wanted suitable (in other words, magnificent) buildings. Many Baroque buildings in Dresden were commissioned by him. They all have a certain lightness and gaiety in common, but the high point of Augustus the Strong's passion for architecture was undoubtedly the Zwinger.

The Zwinger is not a castle in the literal sense of the word, and was never seen as such. It was originally planned as a forecourt to a larger building which was, in fact, never built. Augustus wanted to create a suitably splendid setting for the theatrical performances, tournaments and equestrian events of which he was particularly fond. An open-air theater was the Elector's idea. He commissioned the court architect Matthäus Daniel Pöppelmann to draw up plans for the project and the artist Balthasar Permoser, who had worked in Italy, to supervise the sculptural details. The two artists could not have worked together in a more harmonious manner.

The term "Zwinger" usually refers to the outer bailey of a castle, the area between two defensive walls or earthworks, and it was a very important way of improving a fortress's defensive capability, particularly before the invention of firearms. It could also be used for competitions or as an animal enclosure. The Dresden Zwinger was built on top of the earthworks of the Luna bastion and was named after it, although it was itself never designed as a defensive structure.

It was here that Pöppelmann began building an orangery for Augustus the Strong in 1710, consisting of two pavilions linked by a arcaded gallery. It was only between 1714 and 1716 that the famous Rampart Pavilion and the Long Gallery with the Crown Gate were built. The rest of the building was erected in 1718 as a symmetrical mirror image, first in wood, and then in stone between 1723 and 1728. Because there was no room outside the Zwinger

RIGHT
View of the Rampart Pavilion and part of the festival square ▶

FOLLOWING DOUBLE SPREAD
The Crown Gate forms the main entrance to the Zwinger palace, flanked on each side by arcade galleries ▶▶

◀ **LEFT**
Visitors admiring old paintings in Zwinger museum

◀ **LEFT**
Plaster known as 'herm'
from the Rampart
Pavilion

for any gardens, formal beds were laid out inside the courtyard, which was 380 ft wide and 669 ft long, while the festival ground occupied the center of the area. It is surprising that the Zwinger is such an aesthetically harmonious complex since it was built over such a long period. During the time of its construction, Pöppelmann traveled throughout Europe, particularly in Vienna, Rome and Paris, to find inspiration. He not only emulated what he found but succeeded in developing his own personal interpretation of Baroque architecture.

A bridge across the moat leads to the Crown Gate, which is the main entrance. Columns and pilasters support this edifice, a combination of gate and triumphal arch. It is surmounted by a copper roof shaped like the imperial crown, decorated with gilt motifs and a smaller dazzling gilt crown on top. The magnificence and richness of the gate indicate the residence of a mighty ruler, a haughty hint that appropriate behavior is required of the visitor.

The long, one-story galleries on both sides of the gate seen to bow in deference to this splendor. However, the tall windows flanked by pilasters and decorated with cherubs and vases belie this. When seen from the courtyard, the galleries appear slightly higher because of the plinth. The corner pavilions at either end have two floors but retain the rhythmic style of the galleries. The terraces in front of the corner pavilions can be reached by elegant staircases, one of Pöppelmann's specialities.

The most magnificent part of the Zwinger is the Rampart Pavilion, situated to the west and built against the slope. Constructed like a skeleton frame, there are no solid walls and it has large windows set between pilastered columns. "Hercules Saxonicus" stands on the facade, holding the globe. This is the highest point of the Zwinger, a fact that was undoubtedly deliberate. The connection between Augustus the Strong and Hercules Saxonicus holding the globe becomes obvious in another Herculean figure that represents Augustus. Carvings and statues of many mythological gods and heroes adorn the Zwinger in honor of the Elector.

The carillon pavilion is situated next to the Rampart Pavilion, on level ground and therefore lower down, as a kind of precious pendant. Although Pöppelmann had already planned the carillon, with bells made from Meissen porcelain, for the courtyard facade of this building, it was only added when the Zwinger was restored in the 1930s. It is still chiming today.

The Nymphenbad or nymphaeum, which was the part least damaged during World War II, is situated between the art gallery and the Rampart Pavilion. The Nymphenbad takes its name from the nymphs in the niches, which together with the pool, waterworks and sculptures give this little courtyard a festive atmosphere. All the original sculptures were by Balthasar Permoser. They were skilfully restored by Georg Wrba after the war.

The Zwinger was so badly damaged during the bombing of Dresden in 1945 that it seemed impossible that it could be rebuilt. But reconstruction started only a few weeks after the end of the war and by 1964 the Zwinger was the first historic building to be completely restored in Dresden. Today it houses several museums.

BELVEDERE, VIENNA

Many call it "Vienna's most delicate flower of Baroque architecture" while others see this two-storied stone building as a statement of power by the architect Prince Eugéne of Savoy. In any case, the two palaces set in a large park are the most beautiful Baroque ensemble in Vienna and among the most striking in Europe.

The commander, diplomat and conqueror of the Turks, Prince Eugéne of Savoy (1663–1736), was a man of high standing in Vienna. He was culturally very versatile, highly educated and interested in the arts. His enormous private wealth enabled him to acquire a large collection of valuable works of art. He was also able to indulge his architectural fancies, building the Belvedere in Vienna as a summer residence to add to his winter palace in the town and his hunting lodge in Marchfeld. The Belvedere's elevated site with its wonderful view of the imperial residence, the Hofburg, was undoubtedly a great source of pleasure to him.

The Belvedere consists of two castles, the Upper Belvedere which was used as a pleasure palace for social and festive occasions and the Lower Belvedere, used as a summer residence for Prince Eugéne. The Lower Belvedere was built first, between 1714 and 1716 under the guidance of the architect Johann Lukas von Hildebrandt. The long, elongated building with its single floor is broken up by tall windows, framed by columns that make it look higher. A centrally placed, projecting, two-storied entrance hall gives the building a clear structure. The roof is divided into three parts, emphasizing the central part, and providing the space for a beautiful balustrade adorned with statues, which also creates an elegant link with the sides. In strong contrast with the sumptuous decoration of the interior, this comparatively simple exterior is like a prologue or overture to the Upper Belvedere.

The 1,640 ft of the Belvedere gardens stretching upwards from the Lower Belvedere to the Upper Belvedere enhance this impression. The French garden architect Dominique Girard, designer of the gardens of Versailles, created a Baroque garden with pools, flights of steps and cascades with sculptures of angels and mythical figures – subjects of particular interest to Prince Eugéne. Unfortunately, only parts of this design have been preserved. However, the grandiose climb along the axial orientation of the garden towards the Upper Belvedere remains as imposing as it was in the 18th century, with the graduation of the steps and cascades mirroring the roof line and the reflection of the palace in the pool of water in front,

RIGHT
One of the many statues at the Belvedere ▶

FOLLOWING DOUBLE SPREAD
The mythical sculptures in the gardens of the Upper Belvedere symbolize the warlike bravery and statesmanship of Prince Eugène ▶▶

◀ LEFT
Ceiling painting in the main bedroom of the Lower Belvedere. The theme of Apollo extends through all paintings in the palace

like a final crowning of the palace's magnificence. On turning round, having walked up the garden to the terrace of the Upper Belvedere, there is a breathtaking view of Vienna below. The Upper Belvedere, erected between 1721 and 1723, is also the work of Hildebrandt. There are strong stylistic references to the Lower Belvedere, which have been expanded and increased. It is an elongated, slightly compact building with a projecting central part, and an extra story over two-thirds of the whole width. The graduated roof line has balustrades adorned with statues. The building has four sides with octagonal domed pavilions at the corners, reminiscent of the round towers in Renaissance castles. The decoration of the facade is much more exotic and fanciful than that of the Lower Belvedere.

The interior is decorated with Italian frescoes representing mythological themes. Carlo Carlone painted the walls and ceilings of the Garden Room on the ground floor with scenes depicting the mythological figures of Apollo and Aurora. The Gold Cabinet in the northwest pavilion is resplendent in white and gold decoration, and is embellished with an equestrian statue of Prince Eugéne, made in 1862 by Anton Dominik Fernkorn.

The Marble Room on the first floor is decorated with red marble and stucco, while the paintings on the ceiling represent the "Allegory of Fame." It was in this room that the Austrian State Treaty was signed in 1955. This treaty dealt with the withdrawal of the allied occupation and is seen as the birth of the Second Republic, which still exists today.

◀ **Left**
Magnificent stucco decoration adorns the staircase of the Upper Belvedere

Following double spread
Today, sculptures from the Middle Ages and the baroque period are exhibited in the historic rooms of the Lower Belvedere ▶▶

The Belvedere museums

Both the Upper Belvedere and the Lower Belvedere are now the property of the State and are used as museums devoted mainly to Austrian art. The Lower Belvedere houses the Austrian Baroque museum with Austrian painting and sculpture from 1683 to 1780, including the "Apotheosis of Prince Eugéne" by Balthasar Permoser, commissioned by Prince Eugéne himself. The Baroque museum leads to the Orangery and the Museum of Medieval Art, whose exhibits include woodcuts and paintings on wooden panels. The Upper Belvedere houses the 19th and 20th century Austrian Gallery, which is also well worth seeing. The collections cover several periods, including Classicism, Biedermeier, Romanticism, Impressionism and Expressionism. Many famous artists are represented, such as Caspar David Frederick, Carl Spitzweg, Lovis Corinth, Max Liebermann, Eugéne Delacroix, Auguste Rodin, Claude Monet, Auguste Renoir, Paul Cézanne, Gustav Klimt ("The Kiss"), Egon Schiele ("Tod und Mädchen") and Oscar Kokoschka.

FESTUNG HOHENSALZBURG

The symbol of Mozart's city, the fortress of Hohensalzburg is also the largest fully preserved fortress in central Europe. It was built over 900 years ago. The fortress has never been conquered by force of arms, but in recent years it has had to capitulate under the ever-increasing onslaught of tourists.

In 1075, a power struggle began between the Papacy and the Holy Roman Empire regarding the conferring of titles. Over the course the controversy, Gebhart von Salzburg, a loyal supporter of the pope, built several fortresses on his territory in 1077 including Hohensalzburg. Archbishop Konrad I (1106–47) completed the fortifications that were later instituted and extended in the 15th and 16th centuries. This was because the archbishops had retreated there during the farmers' uprising. The fortress was given its present appearance by Archbishop Leonhard von Keutschach (1495–1519). As a result, his coat of arms (consisting of a beetroot against a black background) is still to be seen at the fortress of Hohensalzburg. Since 1892, a funicular railway has been taking visitors up the hill to the fortress, but those who choose to go on foot will become aware of two important aspects of the fortress: first, its great size, and second, how difficult it must have been for the enemy to attack it. During the Thirty Years War, the enemy had to get past three ramparts with bastions or towers before reaching the castle moat, which could be crossed only by a drawbridge before 1835. A traverse

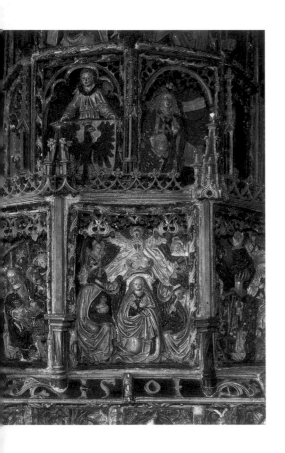

was encountered first, guarded from above and below by the Nonnberg bastion, before reaching the outer bailey. Past the Schüttkasten and workhouse, through the Geyer Tower are the Hasengraben bastions with gun casemates and powder magazine (both have been converted into guest houses today). What today provides a magnificent view of the town for tourists gave the defenders the reassuring knowledge that the attacker could be detected in good time and that they could fire at them with ease. In addition, all the trees growing below the fortress were cut down to make sure that no invaders could use them for cover. The Geyer Gate leads into the castle courtyard with the chaplain's quarters, a large lime-tree and an octagonal, red marble cistern.

Until the 19th century, a deeper moat, carved from the rock and crossed by a drawbridge, guarded the inner castle with round towers, making it a fortress within a fortress. It was only after crossing this moat that the inner castle courtyard with its bakery, kitchens and Hohen Stock, as the inner castle is called, could be captured. It is, therefore, no wonder that the Hohensalzburg fortress has never been captured in its long history.

RIGHT
The Hohensalzburg fortress set high above the Kollegienkirche and the Franciscan church in the foreground ▶

◀ **LEFT**
A decoratively tiled stove in the "Golden Room"

Burg Kufstein

The Kufstein fortress was recorded as early as 1205 when it was under the rule of the bishopric of Regensburg. After Kufstein was awarded the status of a town by the Bavarians in 1393, the fortress built on a steep rocky outcrop was rebuilt in Gothic style in 1415 and enlarged to make it apparently impregnable.

Eleven years later, Emperor Maximilian I was forced to conquer his own 'impregnable' fortress. During the Landshut War of Succession, Maximilian annexed the Bavarian and Tyrolean regions along the Inn River, including Kufstein. However, the commander of the fortress, Hans von Pienzenau, had sided with the Wittelbachs and was therefore opposed to the emperor, who was forced to lay siege to the fortress. It was only when the fortress was attacked by the two largest cannons in Germany that Piezenau gave up. He was beheaded in front of the emperor.

Maximilian renovated the fortress and extended the massive Kaiserturm or emperor's tower in 1518–19. It had a tournament room and fencing room on the first floor, a gun emplacement above and above that a series of cells which served as a state prison between 1778 and 1865. Together with the two smaller towers and the round tower, Maximilian built the most important part of the fortress overlooking the town.

The fortress was enlarged in the 17th century. It then came into use as a more modern military fortress, on which the newest guns could also go into action. It was now equipped with several batteries and an arrow-shaped offshore bastion with casemates, the so-called Josefsburg. However, although the Kufstein fortress was so well secured, its fate was not. The Bavarians conquered and held it from 1703 until 1805, until the fortress became Austrian again in 1814.

RIGHT
Inside the massive Kaiserturm or Emperor Tower on the right of the castle were a tournament area, gun emplacements and, from 1775 to 1865, a number of state prison cells ▶

◀ LEFT
Secret tunnel in Burg Kufstein

SCHLOSS MIRABELL

The mayor of Salzburg is a very fortunate and enviable person, because his workplace is probably one of the most beautiful in Europe. His offices are in Schloss Mirabell, as are those of the Salzburg city council. Schloss Mirabell is situated on the north bank of the Salzach River, with a wonderful view of the city. It is surrounded by the Mirabell garden, a gem of Baroque garden design.

Prince-Archbishop Wolf Dietrich von Raitenau built the castle in 1606 as a gift for his mistress and life-companion, Salome Alt, the daughter of a middle-class family. At this time, it was situated just outside the town. However nothing remains of this original Schloss Altenau but the garden, and the magnificent site overlooking the old town towards the fortress of Hohensalzburg (see page 128). His competitive cousin and successor, Markus Sittikus von Hohenems, immediately changed the name to Schloss Mirabell in order to obliterate all memory of Prince-Archbishop Wolf Dietrich and his beloved. Count von Lodron, on the other hand, who was prince-archbishop of Salzburg from 1619 until 1653, lived and died in the castle and linked it to the town by building a series of bulwarks. (Mirabell is situated in the center of Salzburg, surrounded by the city.) Between 1721 and 1727, the castle was entirely rebuilt in Baroque style with the addition of a striking tower crowned by a cupola according to a design by Johann Lukas von Hildebrandt. However, in 1818, barely a hundred years later, much of Salzburg was destroyed by fire – including the magnificent Schloss Mirabell.

In 1819, Peter de Nobile, the chief court architect and director of the Vienna School of Architecture, was entrusted with the task of rebuilding the castle. Because he wanted to interpret contemporary architecture rather than restore old architecture, he rebuilt Mirabell in classical style, less decorated and more sober than its 18th century Baroque predecessor, giving it its present appearance.

Three-storied wings surround a square courtyard. The two main facades overlooking the Mirabellplatz are embellished with magnificent balconies, as is the rear garden facade. Details such as the window surrounds, capitals and stuccowork recall Mirabell's past Baroque magnificence. In addition, the present castle still boasts three splendid relics of the original Baroque castle in the shape of the staircase, marble hall and castle church, all of which survived the fire.

The hall with its ceiling decorated with stucco dating from the early Rococo period leads to the "angels' staircase," a superb achievement of by Lukas von Hildebrandt.

RIGHT
The entwined balustrade of the marble staircase decorated with cherubs ▶

FOLLOWING DOUBLE SPREAD
Schloss Mirabell in its baroque garden setting ▶▶

◀ LEFT
Pegasus Fountain in the Schloss Mirabell gardens

This monumental marble staircase has a wonderfully intricate banister, decorated with reclining or seated cherubs, leading up the stairs to the marble hall, now used for weddings. The sculptures in the niches in the walls are by Georg Raphael Donner. Hermann Bahr wrote about this staircase: "I know of no other stairs that arouse such a feeling of sensual well-being when climbing them." If the Austrian author was so impressed, one may imagine how a bride and groom will feel when climbing this grandiose staircase, on their way to be married in the grance marble hall to which it leads. This beautiful wedding hall has an atmosphere of magnificence and pomp with its smooth walls of white, red-veined marble, embellished with fine, gilt lines forming decorative motifs and punctuated by pilasters. Further ornament is provided by a green marble mantelpiece, gold medallions and a sparkling glass chandelier. As well as being a place where fashionable couples get married, this breathtaking former banqueting hall of the castle is also a magical setting for concerts.

A rather nondescript side gate leads from Mirabellenplatz to the castle church which has a charming interior with stucco marble walls embellished with fluted pilasters, and an elegant pink and gray marble altar, surmounted by a gilt, latticed baldachin capped with a crown.

Almost more famous than the castle is the Mirabell garden, which has preserved its original Baroque layout without the revolutionary changes that the castle has undergone. There are fountains, water basins, stone balustrades and vases, sculptures and groups of figures, cone-shaped box topiary and floral arabesques. Two lions guard the entrance to the bulwark garden, which contains the so-called "dwarf garden." Stone dwarfs and grotesque figures with hunchbacks, goitres and smirking faces can be seen standing on a little square and amongst the shrubbery. They represent curious situations or Salzburg eccentrics. Crown Prince Ludwig of Bavaria found them so disturbing that he wanted to destroy them when he was living at Mirabell for a time. In fact, many of them were sold at auction at one point, but they were later bought back and again placed in the dwarf garden.

Nearby are two equally characteristic features of Baroque gardens: a small maze and an open-air theater. This open-air theater is the oldest north of the Alps, and was actually used for theatrical performances. The hedges are in the shape of stage wings, where actors wait to make their entrance onto the stage. There is even an orchestra pit in front of the stage, surrounded by greenery. It was used to stage pantomimes, operas and ballets.

The prince-bishop and the citizen-daughter

Prince-Bishop Wolf Dietrich of Raitenau, who became archbishop of Salzburg at the age of 28, fell in love with Salome Alt, the daughter of a highly respectable Salzburg merchant. They had fifteen children, ten of whom survived. It is unknown whether Wolf Dietrich ever "married" his beloved to relieve her conscience.

Schloss Schönbrunn

A monument to the Habsburgs, an imperial summer residence, the center of European politics, the home of Maria Theresa and the Empress Sissi, and a center of the arts, Schloss Schönbrunn is a remarkable combination of architecture and garden art, illustrating the transition from Baroque to Rococo, and one of the most important architectural sites in Europe.

This palace is situated to the southwest of the Austrian capital Vienna, in the district of Hietzing. It was named after a "beautiful spring," known for its particularly pure water. The present palace was erected on the site of an older building destroyed by the Turks in 1683. Emperor Leopold I (1640–1705) entrusted Johann Bernhard Fischer von Erlach with the task of building an imposing palace for his son Joseph I, which was intended to surpass Versailles, the palace of his enemy, Louis XIV in splendor. However, this proved an impossible task because the enormous building costs vastly exceeded the financial means of Leopold I. In 1696, building started on a scaled-down version of Fischer von Erlach's plans, which is still very imposing today, and certainly left its mark on both the emperor's purse and that of his successor.

The work dragged on and the Habsburgs lived on a building site for a long time. It was only under Maria Theresa (1717–80) that any real progress was made. She commissioned Nikolau Pacassi to rework and extend Fischer's plans because she wanted to live there with her husband – the Emperor Franz I – and their sixteen children, as well as with with the numerous members of their court. This entourage consisted of 56 butchers, eleven priests and nine doctors as well as about 1,000 officials, ministers, servants and ladies-in-waiting.

Pacassi toned down the majestic pomposity of Baroque and introduced the sophisticated lightness of Rococo, especially in the decoration of the interior. These typical Rococo features included playful "rocaille"

RIGHT
The Neptune fountain in the center of the park. Thetis is begging for help from her son Achilles from Neptune, god of the sea ▶

FOLLOWING DOUBLE SPREAD
It was originally intended that Schönbrunn should surpass Versailles, but in reality there was only enough money for a reduced version. Even so the result was impressive ▶▶

◀ **LEFT**
Dining room in Schloss Schönbrunn

◀ **LEFT**
The impressive palm
house for tender plants
in the gardens of
Schönbrunn

shapes, mirrors and paintings on the wall. In addition, a few of the rooms were decorated with chinoiserie motifs, which were highly fashionable at the time. The Little Gallery is flanked by the Oval Cabinet on one side and the Round Cabinet on the other. Lacquer panels of various sizes and shapes have been inserted in the white wood paneling. Small consoles, used to display blue and white china, complete the gilt frames. Both galleries were originally designed as banqueting halls and were therefore decorated with magnificent stuccowork and frescoes and are now considered the most important Rococo creations of imperial residential architecture. The frescoes were painted by Gregorio Guglielmi between 1755 and 1761, while the stucco that followed in 1761–63 was by Albert Bolla.

On 11 November 1918, in the Blue Chinese Salon, Charles I renounced all claim to govern under the auspices of the Austro-Hungarian Empire. The next day the Austrian Republic was proclaimed. This also signaled the end of Schönbrunn as imperial residence of the Habsburgs.

Forty of the 1,000 or more rooms of the palace are now open to the public. These rooms illustrate the various needs of the palace inhabitants in days gone by, ranging from the lantern room where servants were on call with lanterns, to the banqueting room in the Great Gallery. Most of the interior decoration and furnishings are still original.

The large wrought-iron main gate leads into the main courtyard, formed by the palace with its central projection and wings to the right and left, the castle theater and the puppet theater with the former stable buildings adjoining on each side, as well as the Wagenburg to the west and the Orangerie to the east. In all, the complex is over 875 yards long.

Behind the palace is a park designed in the French style by Johann Ferdinand Hetzendorff in the 1770s. The visual axis leads from the garden facade to the imposing Neptune fountain, in the center of which Thetis kneels as she begs the mighty figure with the Trident to help her son Achilles during his sea voyage. The view up the hill is of the Gloriette, where Fischer had originally planned to erect the palace. This classical arcade was built between 1772 and 1775 to commemorate the victory over the Prussians near Kolin in 1757. The central part is now glassed in and houses a café that is very popular because of its magnificent view of Schönbrunn and Vienna. The gardens on both side of this visual axis are symmetrically laid out. On each side is a Naiad Fountain towards which the paths, arranged in a star shape, converge. There are numerous statues of mythological figures. To the west is the Schönbrunn zoological garden, designed by Jean Nicolas Jadot de Ville-Issey and opened in 1752. The circular arrangement was inspired by the zodiac, with its central Baroque pavilion (built in 1759) and twelve surrounding "lodges" used as animal enclosures.

The neighboring palm house was designed by Franz Xaver Sengenschmidt. Built in 1882, it is a brilliant achievement of engineering skill with its iron structure 360 ft long and 98 ft wide. It is still is one of the largest greenhouses in Europe. Schönbrunn among others has a Children's Museum where kids can experience what it's like to be a 'emperor's child'.

SCHLOSS TRATZBERG

Schloss Tratzberg, one of the most important castles in north Tyrol, is situated in a picturesque location overlooking the Inn valley on the eastern slope of the Karwendel Mountains. The most fascinating feature of this building is its homogenous architecture, reflecting the transition between Gothic and Renaissance, as well as other architectural styles incorporated in later additions.

High on a hill near the municipality of Jenbach in the Austrian province of Tyrol, schloss Tratzberg was built on the site of a fortress dating from 1296 when the border with Bavaria still ran through this point. After a fire had destroyed the tower and the two wings containing the living quarters, the Tänzl brothers replaced the fortress with a completely new castle. The next owner, Georg Ilsung, extended the castle while preserving the building plan of the original, which was based on an almost square ground plan consisting of an inner courtyard surrounded by four wings with two or three stories. The south wing is flanked by two slender towers, with the left one slightly taller than the building itself. A third tower projects in the center of the facade. There is a wonderful view of the Inn valley to the west from the terrace in front of the main gate.

The inner courtyard contains an elegant spiral staircase to wer. There is a harmonious interplay of pilasters and arcades along the north wing and superimposed arcades along the south wing. The interior with its ceilings supported by wooden beams, beautiful ironwork and metal fittings gives an impression of solidity and prosperity. The Habsburg hall is particularly interesting be cause it is a perfect example of German Re naissance. Only a single column of red marble supports the vast ceiling. There is a fresco 151 ft long of a family tree depicting the 148 ancestors of Emperor Maxi milian I.

RIGHT:
The inner courtyard, where the transition from Gothic to Renaissance style can be seen ▶

◀ **LEFT**
Schloss Tratzberg

Festung Munot

Most visitors come to the city of Schaffhausen simply to admire the famous Rhine Falls in the Swiss capital of the canton of the same name. But the city has another symbol and distinctive feature of great interest: Festung Munot, the only example of the practical application of Dürer's theories on fortress architecture.

Albrecht Dürer is best known as a painter, but he was also interested in military matters. He wrote a book on forts, published in Nuremberg in 1527, in which he developed his theory that a circular fort was the most effective for defensive purposes. His reasoning was that a round fortress made it possible to drive back attacks from any direction by all-round defense. Because of Schaffhausen's strategic location on the Rhine, a new round fortress was designed to be built on the site of an older building and to meet all modern military requirements. The people of Schaffhausen also wanted the building to reflect their municipal pride. Discussions dragged on for much of the 16th century and building did not start until 1564. It was only completed in 1589, and in the quarter of a century taken to build it, the defensive technology of the Munot fortress became almost obsolete.

Walls 16 feet thick enclose the round fortress, which contains spacious casemates. Four substantial round pillars support the vault of the casemates, lit by special shafts through which the light penetrates. Above is an open platform for the artillery and soldiers. This parapet was enclosed by a covered gangway in 1622. To the south is the tall round tower with a spiral ramp to enable soldiers and weapons to reach the platform as well as riders and their horses. The guards were accommodated in the distinctive octagonal upper floor, with its steeply pitched tiled roof. In addition to the moat that surrounds the sober fortress, it is further protected to the north by three small bastions. Although Festung Munot was technically obsolete as soon as it was finished, it actually fulfilled its role successfully for over 200 years. It was only occupied once, by the French in 1799, when they were fleeing from the Austrians. As the city fortification became totally ineffective a few years later, the fortress fell into disrepair and was used as a quarry, until a private restoration project began in 1826.

The hill on which Festung Munot stands is used as vineyard today. Pinot-Gris and Tokay grapes are grown there, and depending on the weather 7,000 to 9,000 bottles of Munötler wine are produced each year.

RIGHT
Festung Munot, the round defensive fortress set high above the city of Schaffhausen ▶

◀ **LEFT**
The spriral ramp to enable soldiers to reach the platform with their weapons and horses

BLOIS

The chateau of Blois stands on a hill between the valleys of two rivers: the Loire and the Arrou. The oldest parts of the chateau date from the 13th century while the most recent addition is the southwest wing, added in 1635. The chateau of Blois is therefore a perfect illustration of the development of French architecture over a period of 400 years.

In the 13th century, the count of Blois built a medieval fortress of which the only surviving parts today are the Tour du Foix with its magnificent views over the historic center of Blois, and the corner building of the chateau containing the Salle des États. The name of this room comes from the fact that under Henry III the States General (the government assembly) met here in 1576 and 1588. The impressive room is divided by arcades with pointed arches and columns.

When Louis XII was crowned king in 1498, he chose Blois as the royal capital because he had been born in the city in 1462 and had inherited the chateau. He immediately enlarged the existing building and made it L-shaped with the addition of a two-story wing in late Gothic style. Above the round, arched doorway that leads to the inner courtyard stands an equestrian statue of Louis XII by Charles Seurre, made in 1857 to replace an earlier statue destroyed during the French Revolution. The inner courtyard has staircase towers in the corners and an elegant covered walkway that links this part of the brick and stone building to the chapel of Saint Calais. Louis XII built this chapel with a single aisle, but it was largely replaced in the 17th century by a new building, the Gaston d'Orléans wing. Today only the elegant chancel of the chapel (built in 1508) has survived. The windows include stained glass by Max Ingrand (1957) depicting events that have marked the history of the castle.

The Louis XII wing is now occupied by the "Musée des Beaux-Arts", which includes paintings, tapestries and costumes from the 17th, 18th and 19th centuries. The history of the architectural development of the chateau of Blois continues with King François I. Having married Louis XII's daughter, he succeeded Louis XII after the latter's death in 1515 and continued the enlargement of the chateau by adding the stunning northwest wing, which has survived almost intact. Although only 15 years separate the parts built by Louis XII and François I, all traces of the late Gothic style have disappeared, replaced by the Renaissance in all its splendor.

Surviving parts of the old medieval fortifications have been incorporated into the new buildings, including the walls separating the courtyard from the city itself. The new first part of the chateau faces the interior courtyard. It has a delightful facade, embellished with pilasters, decorated with Italianate ornament and crowned with pierced eaves and roof windows, giving the building an elegant, harmonious appearance. Especially remarkable is the

RIGHT
The magnificent chimneypiece on the first floor of the François I wing of the chateau4
▶

FOLLOWING DOUBLE SPREAD
The Louis XII wing. During his reign, Blois became the capital of France for a number of years ▶▶

projecting open spiral staircase tower. A stroke of genius on the part of the architect, it combines several functions. It is a spectacular decorative feature of the main facade, it acts as a staircase linking the three floors of this wing, and it also serves as a balcony for watching theatrical performances in the courtyard.

François I felt that the rooms of this wing of the chateau were insufficiently impressive and spacious. He therefore added a spectacular external facade above the old surrounding walls, with a gallery on the first floor and many other rooms. This Loggia Facade has a picturesque arrangement of galleries, pilasters, bay windows, loggias and balconies, as well as many decorative elements and royal emblems. With this impressive new wing, Blois was no longer a mere fortress, but a chateau that symbolized François I's divine right.

In the 17th century Louis XIII's brother Gaston d'Orléans was named Count of Blois, and he commissioned the architect François Mansart to build him a new chateau befitting his position. The plans would have involved the demolition of the existing buildings, but these plans were curtailed when it became apparent that the funds available were inadequate. A new southwest wing was built between 1635 and 1638, and only those buildings that stood in its way were demolished.

The most recent addition to the chateau, the three-story Gaston d'Orléans wing, was built in French Renaissance style. In spite of the difficulty of the task, Mansart tried to create a symmetrical ensemble, consisting of a slightly projecting central section flanked by bays and short side wings looking onto the courtyard, linked by curved arcades of coupled columns at each corner. The facade is clearly articulated with pilasters and other repeated decorative elements. Because of the lack of funds, the rooms inside were not finished, and even the stairs were only completed in 1932.

Balzac's admiration for the staircase tower

In his novel Catherine de Médicis, Honoré de Balzac described the staircase tower of the chateau of Blois: "This vertiginous creation, whose brilliantly delicate, miraculous details seem to make the stones speak, can only be compared to the fine, richly carved ivory masterpieces from China or Dieppe. In other words, the stone resembles the finest silk lace. The flowers, the figures and the animals that cling to the sides of the stairs seem to multiply with every step, culminating at the top in vaulted stonework where the chisel of 16th century art has sought to excel the naive sculptors who 50 years earlier had carved the stones of the staircases in the Louis XII wing."

◀ **LEFT**
The famous staircase tower. It was described in a novel by Balzac, among others

Carcassonne

"Important from an art historical and archaeological point of view... a unique complex and the most remarkable model of medieval military history." Thus did Prosper Mérimée describe the town of Carcassonne in 1850 in a letter to the war ministry explaining the importance of restoring it. It is thanks to him that this magnificent fortress has been preserved.

The Gauls recognized that the narrow corridor on the Aude River linking the Mediterranean and the Atlantic was a strategically important site and they established a settlement, "Carcasso", there. This was later developed into a castellum by the Romans and further fortified into a bastion by the Visigoths in the 5th century. Coveted from earliest times for its strategic significance, Carcassonne has had a very checkered history. The fortress was erected in 1130 and the Romanesque cathedral of Saint-Nazaire was built twenty years later. It was only in the mid-13th century, under the rule of the French kings, that the town was systematically fortified. A second, mile-long circle of defensive walls, including the Porte Narbonnaise and watch towers, was built around the original town walls to increase security. When weapons using gunpowder were invented, the town's defenses were increased by the construction of a circular crenelated barbican to the west, to protect both the castle and access to the river Aude. The church of St Gimer was built on the site.

The construction of the fortifications lasted well into the 14th century but Carcassonne had already ceased to be the scene of conflicts and clashes. As a result, the fortified town lost its defensive role, especially since the inhabitants had moved to the other bank of the Aude and built a new town under royal administration. (They had been driven out of the fortified town and settled at its foot; this settlement was destroyed by Louis the Pious in 1240.) While the new town grew into what is today the capital of the département of Aude in southern France, the old upper town went into rapid decline.

It was only when the author Prosper Mérimée became fascinated with France's historical medieval monument that Carcassonne came back into the limelight. It was reconstructed by Viollet-le-Duc in the mid-19th century. In the romantic climate of the time, buildings were not always restored to their exact original condition; they were often "put right" or "perfected" from an aesthetic and didactic point of view. Restoration brought life back to the old fortified town so that at the beginning of the 20th century it was a favorite stopping-place for travelers on their way to Biarritz or the Riviera. Mass tourism put Carcassonne back on the map, and anyone wanting to visit this peaceful fortified town should do so out of season. If visiting in the tourist season, the best time is early in the morning or in the evening when the town is at its best, bathed in the soft light of the low sun.

RIGHT
The Chateau Comtal inside Carcassonne ▶

FOLLOWING DOUBLE SPREAD
View on the impressive walls and watchtowers of Carcassonne ▶▶

BELOW
Interior of the castle ▼

Chambord

Even when the chateau of Chambord was still being built, Emperor Charles V praised it in the highest terms. In 1539, he called it "the quintessence of everything that human art is capable of producing." In spite of all its magnificence, the building is still uncompleted, but even so the verdict is virtually the same: Chambord is the high point of Renaissance architecture on the Loire.

François I wanted a representative palace, a perfect edifice, the embodiment of his reign as a worthy, perfect king. His love of hunting must have been uppermost in his mind when he selected Sologne, rich in woods and game, as the site. François I had about 13,600 acres enclosed by a wall 20 miles long. Today this park is accessible to ordinary mortals, and deer and wild boar thrive in it as before.

The king had the existing medieval castle torn down and built a new one, just 10 miles from Blois and 3 miles kilometers from the Loire. At first glance it might seem that the unknown architect had created something completely original for the time, but that would be a false impression: the floor plan is similar to that of feudal fortresses of the Middle Ages, and thus has its roots in France's constructional heritage. A keep, the traditional living tower in medieval fortresses, forms the center of Chambord, while round towers at each corner make it an impressive fortress in its own right. Emperor Charles V, incidentally, only saw this part of the castle completed. Similar towers are at the other corners of the square, terminating the connecting wings of the building, because for all its splendor, security remained a priority.

The fact that Chambord does not give the impression of a being a medieval fortress, but rather a Renaissance palace, is due to its regular arrangement and to its playful decoration. Cornices and pilasters sub-divide the surfaces of the walls in a clear rhythm. Windows and arcades follow an unhurried sequence which could quickly have become boring were it not broken by the roof with its richly decorated and highly varied lanterns and chimneys. There are round and square turrets with pointed roofs or spires, and chimneys decorated with geometric shapes, fabulous creatures and flowers. Everywhere there are lilies, crowns and the capital letter F for François I, King of France.

The roof terrace is reached from a central spiral staircase in the Italian style with two flights, which may have been designed by Leonardo da Vinci. Despite the well-organized floor plan, the 440 rooms in Chambord make the chateau a real labyrinth, partly because there are so many of them, but also because of a multitude of corridors and galleries, stairs and curves and ante-chambers. Part of the chateau is open to visitors today, but all the original furniture and fixtures that could be moved were either plundered or auctioned off during the French Revolution. The building was no longer inhabited at the time, and to those who believed in

Right
Alcoved bed in one of the 18th century apartments ▶

Following double spread
Although unfinished, the chateau is undeniably impressive as an example of Renaissance architecture in the Loire region ▶▶

"Liberty, Equality, Fraternity", it was an eyesore, if solely on principle. The only thing that saved this "great pile of worthless bricks" for future generations was the frightening cost of demolishing it. Some of the rooms have been refurbished with an eye to preservation, and indeed each is decorated in the style of the various inhabitants of the chateau and their times.

Tribute is paid to François I and his enthusiasms in a hall with a series of tapestries that tell "the hunting stories of François I", and in a bedroom with a red canopy bed. The King was a ladies' man, and he supposedly scratched the words "A woman's mind changes often" on the windowpane in this room with a diamond ring. Louis XIV is said to have discovered this "graffito" together with Maria Mancini and, being the perfect gentleman, shattered the pane. An apartment with a showpiece room was designed for the Sun King, who reveled in the lively parties and hunting at Chambord. Rooms were also set aside for the Duc de Chambord. It is said that he only spent two nights here, but it is thanks to him that the palace was restored in the 19th century.

The incomplete beauty

Although Chambord is one of Europe's most famous buildings, even today historians have not been able to clarify who designed the chateau, or who the architect was. François de Pontbriant took over as general supervisor of the building project on 6 September 1519. Five years later, the campaign in Italy interrupted the construction work for two years. The keep was completed in 1533, and the corner towers and pavilions on the roof were finished four years later. The residence for François I was completed in 1547, not that the new owner saw it very much. He died the same year, but whether (as legend has it) he really only spent 40 days in his palace cannot be conclusively established. His successor Henri II continued the building work, although he did not complete it either. Shortage of funds, the Religious Wars and finally Henry's death in 1559 saw to that. Consequently one tower and two wings remain incomplete to this day. However, this takes nothing away from the breathtaking effect of this superb building.

CHENONCEAU

"Its turrets and square chimneys rise high up in the sky at the end of a long avenue, away from the village ... surrounded by woodland, set in a large park with beautiful lawns, in the middle of the river. The river Cher burbles under the high arches whose sharp edges cut through the water. Its sleekness is both robust and soft at the same time and its melancholy is without boredom or bitterness." This is how Gustave Flaubert (1821-1880) described the chateau of Chenonceau.

Described by many as France's first real Renaissance chateau, Chenonceau is on the river Cher, a tributary of the Loire, near the town of Chenonceaux. Women play a prominent role in the history of the castle. In 1517 the original castle was rebuilt by the royal treasurer Thomas Bohier who bought the property from its impoverished owners, the lords of Marques. He demolished the castle, leaving only the keep, which he modernized and rebuilt in Renaissance style. Because Bohier spent a lot of time in Italy, his wife, Catherine Briçonnet, supervised the building work. Unfortunately, neither of them was able to enjoy the chateau for very long because Thomas died in 1524 and Catherine two years later. The heirs had to cede it to the king because of Thomas's enormous debts to the treasury.

When Henri II came on the throne his long-time mistress, Diane de Poitiers, asked him for the castle. He gave it to her – to the great annoyance of his wife, Catherine de Medicis. Between 1556 and 1559, Diane de Poitiers enlarged the chateau and built the bridge with the five arches across the Cher. She embellished the garden with a fountain nearly 20 ft high, which was quite extraordinary at the time. All this work was financed by the introduction of a "bell tax" on every bell in the kingdom.

When Henri II died in 1559, Catherine de Medicis did not hesitate to remove her archrival from Chenonceau, installing her in the less elegant chateau of Chaumont so she could move into Chenonceau herself. She decided to rebuild it and make it one of the most imposing chateaus in France. However, she was unable to carry out her ambitious plans, probably because of a lack of money, so only the two-storied gallery over the bridge across the Cher (1580), the

RIGHT
Chenonceau is sometimes called the women's chateau, being the favorite residence of queens, favorites and mistresses ▶

FOLLOWING DOUBLE SPREAD
Because of its wonderful garden, the perfection of its architecture and its unique location, Chenonceau is recognized as the most beautiful of the chateaus of the Loire ▶▶

◀ **LEFT**
After removing her archrival from Chenonceau, Catherine de Medicis created a very pretty park

◀ **LEFT**
Catherine de Medicis
organised sumptuous
balls in this great hall
197 ft long, spanning
the whole width of the
river Cher

outbuildings in the forecourt (1580–85), a small extension to the chapel and the rebuilding of the east facade were carried out. The facade was later changed back to its original design. Naturally, Catherine also wanted to have her own park, to the southwest of the castle, which, contrary to expectation, was smaller than that of Diane de Poitiers.

After Catherine's death in 1589, her daughter-in-law, Louise von Lotharingen, the wife of Henri III, inherited the chateau. When the king was murdered later in the year, she went into mourning for the rest of her life; she dressed only in white and painted all the rooms in the chateau black. Chenonceau fell into a long sleep after the death of Louise von Lotharingen. In 1733, it was bought by Claude and Louise Dupin who were passionate patrons of the arts and sciences, and they brought Chenonceau back to life. Louise Dupin invited artists and scholars to her salon, and Jean-Jacques Rousseau was tutor to her children.

Unlike many other castles, Chenonceau was not destroyed or damaged during the French Revolution, probably because it was the only bridge across the river Cher in the region.

Marguerite Pelouze was the next owner of the chateau. She bought it the 19th century and spent her entire fortune renovating it, ruining herself financially. Since 1913, it has belonged to the Menier family.

Built as a moated castle in the middle of the river Cher, Chenonceau is a square building with four round towers at the corners and balconies or terraces embellishing every wing. The views are magnificent from anywhere in the chateau and the exterior is inviting and friend-ly. It was built according to canonical Italian Renaissance style, so that the proportions of the facades and the roof with dormer windows are symmetrical. Only the east side still has traces of irregularity, characteristic of the architecture of François I.

The interior is dominated by a vast, long hall rising across two floors with a ceiling supported by wooden beams. All the adjacent rooms on the ground floor open up onto this large hall, including the so-called Garden room, whose majolica floor has only survived at its edges. As in northern Italian villas, the staircase rises straight up in the center of the hall.

The typically Renaissance galleries were used for festive occasions. The two-storied gal-lery that Catherine built on the bridge, with large fireplaces, wooden ceilings and black-and-white floors, provided ample space to entertain numerous guests, a frequent occurrence. Catherine's parties often lasted several days and were famous because she did not stint on anything, offering her guests spectacular entertainment such as "54 little boats deco-rated with festoons" fighting a "naval battle" to amuse the guests after the meal, or scantily-dressed women to titillate them while eating.

Druyes-les-belles-Fontaines

The fortress of Druyes-les-belles-Fontaines was built almost a thousand years ago on a steep rocky outcrop, about 19 miles south of Auxerre. Today only ruins remain, but it is one of the most important medieval secular buildings in France from an architectural point of view. Interestingly, it was originally built to compete with the Louvre in Paris.

The history of this fortress is closely linked to two members of the French aristocracy. The fortress of Druyes-les-belles-Fontaines in Burgundy was built by Pierre II de Courtenay, a cousin of King Philippe II Auguste. In 1184, Pierre had married Agnés, the daughter of the Count of Nevers and the king's ward. As one of the richest women in the country, she brought vast estates with her as well as the region of Druyes-les-Belles-Fontaines. Together the two cousins went on the Third Crusade (1189–92), achieving glory in the Holy Land. Back in France, they were soon looking for new challenges.

Thus in 1193, each began to build a fortress: the king in his capital, Paris, and his less powerful cousin Pierre at home in Druyes-les-belles Fontaines. Both erected square buildings, protected by massive walls with solid, round towers, a gate tower and two residential wings. This type of fortified castle was an entirely new concept in France at the time, and it is not known what inspired them.

The cousins probably exchanged ideas during the long journey to the Holy Land and perhaps were influenced by fortresses they saw on the way. The result was two very similar fortified castles, built at the same time, which differed mainly because of the site. When building the Louvre in Paris, King Philip II built the first prototype of the early medieval fortified castle set in flat terrain, while his cousin Pierre transposed the same type of building to the top of a hill, undoubtedly an amazing feat of construction.

The fortified castle of Druyes-les-belles-Fontaines was built from large blocks of stone. The imposing ruins include the fortification walls, the massive round towers at the corners and the residential wings with the arched windows, grouped close together. In the middle of the southwest side is a chapel with a ribbed vault ceiling, whose apse is situated in a square side tower.

Access is through the crenelated stone tower gate. This consists of projection parapets supported by corbels, with openings through which objects could be hurled at the assailant. In case of attack, boiling pitch, oil or water could be poured onto the enemy below. A moat between the mountain ridge and the fortress provided further protection. This type of fortress was to become a symbol of power in France, which only the highest-ranking families could afford. The huge, imposing hilltop fortress of Mont-Saint-Jean in the granite mountain region of the Auxois is a well-preserved fortress in the same style.

RIGHT
Built from large blocks of stone, the fortress was the model for many castles in the future ▶

FOLLOWING DOUBLE SPREAD
Pierre II's idea for the fortress of Druyes-les-belles-Fontaines may have come to him during the Third Crusade ▶▶

FONTAINEBLEAU

The magnificent chateau of Fontainebleau, situated in the middle of a forest, is the most perfect early Renaissance chateau in France. This is appropriately reflected in the name of the original entrance gate, which is a clever play on words: the "porte d'orée", the "gate to the edge of the forest", sounds the same as "porte dorée" or "golden gate."

The forest of Fontainebleau, one of the largest and wildest forests in the Île-de-France, is about 37 miles southeast of Paris. Its proximity to the French capital and its rich stock of game made it an ideal hunting-ground for the kings of France. However, traveling such a distance on horseback or by coach was quite strenuous at the time and it was therefore decided to build a hunting lodge in the forest.

The original construction of Fontainebleau dates back to Louis the Pious who in 1259 built a keep and a convent hospital on the site of an old manor house near a spring, called "Fontaine-Belle-Eau", whose name he gave to the keep. Over time, it acquired the typical features of a castle such as fortifications and outbuildings built around a courtyard.

The castle fell into disrepair and King François I decided to rebuild it as a Renaissance chateau, making it his official residence. He appointed a master-builder from Paris – Gilles le Breton – to supervise the construction. In the first phase of building, le Breton built a number of pavilions on the foundations of the old castle: one each for the king, the children and the queen, the gate house with the Porte d'Orée and the stepped pavilion. He also built two superimposed chapels and a ballroom 98 ft long and 33 ft wide, originally planned as a passageway to the chapel of Saint-Saturnin.

The coffered ceiling, the delightful paintings from the School of Fontainebleau and the large fireplace made it ideal for sumptuous banquets and balls. Standing near the fireplace are two bronze statues of satyrs – infamously lascivious and wine-loving devils.

The most artistically important part of Fontainebleau was also built between 1534 and 1537: the François I gallery. It is the earliest example of the long, narrow type of room that became very popular in European palaces and country houses, especially in France and England. Nevertheless, its architectural origin and its original purpose are still unclear. Initially, this passage room was where merchants sold their wares, but it is almost incredible to thinks that such a magnificent, Italianate Renaissance interior should be used for such purposes. The Italian artists Rosso Fiorentino, Niccolò dell'Abbate and Francesco Primatic-

RIGHT
The Musée Napoléon
Napoleon´s throne ▶

FOLLOWING DOUBLE SPREAD
The present, irregular appearance of the chateau is the result of continuous alterations and additions ▶▶

◀ **LEFT**
The gardens and park are a favourite excursion destination by Parisians

cio decorated the upper half of the gallery walls with paintings, stuccowork and sculptures. While the wall paintings exalted the monarchy with allegories on the kingdom, the wood panelling in the lower part was decorated with carvings of coats-of-arms and François I's monogram. The ensemble, a portrayal of the extravagant, lavish life at the court, had a lasting influence on the decoration of French chateaus and is the birthplace of the first School of Fontainebleau.

Primaticcio also decorated the baths that François I built in 1535. Sadly, these luxurious baths with restrooms and steam-baths were demolished to make way for more living quarters in the late 17th century.

After the death of François I, his son Henri II continued enlarging and embellishing Fontainebleau as did subsequent monarchs, especially Henri IV and Louis XV who both contributed to the present appearance of Fontainebleau. The approach to the irregular chateau complex, arranged around five courts, leads to the celebrated horseshoe-shaped double flight of stairs. This was built for Louis XIII in 1643 by Jean Androuet du Cerceau.

Napoleon Bonaparte loved staying at Fontainebleau. He came here to recover from his military campaigns and official duties. He also abdicated here. It was in the Salon Rouge at Fontainebleau that he signed the act of abdication after his defeat in 1814.

He probably walked down the horseshoe-shaped flight of stairs to the "Court of the White Horse" (Cours du Cheval-Blanc) where he said farewell to his guards before going into exile to Elba. Since then, the courtyard has been called the "Cours des Adieux", an unusual name for a courtyard where welcomes outnumber farewells.

◀ **LEFT**
Hunting scenes on the water features in the park remind us of the original purpose of the castle

The Schools of Fontainebleau

The first School of Fontainebleau included the Italians Rosso Fiorentino, Francesco Primaticcio and Niccolò dell'Abbate as well as French artists, all working during the period 1530–60. The second School of Fontainebleau was formed of artists responsible for the interior decoration of the chateau in the late 16th and early 17th century, executing works such as the wall paintings in the Chapelle de la Sainte-Trinité. This second School of Fontainebleau included artists such as Toussaint du Breuil, Martin Fréminet and Ambroise Dubois, who introduced the influence of Flemish art in France. But the first School of Fontainebleau was the most important and pioneering, because it introduced Italian Mannerism in France.

Quéribus and Peyrepertuse

The rocky ridges of Corbières rise precipitously into the sky. The vigilant wind rages across the craggy mountain tops. In spite or rather because it is such an inaccessible place and the surroundings are so inhospitable, these high rocky outcrops, some as high as 2,600 ft, are littered with the ruins of old fortresses: they are the fortresses where the Cathars took refuge.

Aguilar, Padern, Quéribus, Peyrepertuse, Puilaurens, Puivert – the ruins of these old forts stretch out to the west of Perpignan like fortification walls along the almost impassable ridge of the foothills of the Pyrenees. From the road in the valley it is often difficult to distinguish the keeps of these fortresses from the rocky peaks. They were built from the stone of the Corbières mountains and as a result they seem to be part of the rock itself: well-camouflaged and difficult to capture.

Most of these were built as early as the 11th century or even earlier as observation posts on the contested Franco-Spanish border, long before they became the retreat and refuge of Cathars. Because of their high altitude and inaccessibility, few men were needed to defend them. Later King Louis VIII would appreciate their invulnerability.

After winning a decisive battle against the Cathars that brought the south of France under his rule, he converted these keeps into fortresses in the 13th century. This enabled him to reinforce the defense of his new territories and the border with Spain at the same time.

The area covered by the double fortress of Peyrepertuse is about 1,000 ft long. A narrow path leads to the barbican and a small entrance door leads to the lower wall where the sentry was on guard. The church of Sainte-Marie served both as place of worship and of refuge. It was integrated into the main fortress as a keep and chapel, known as the "Old Keep", which was also the entrance to the second line of fortifications. The second fortress of Peyrepertuse, San Jordi, is immediately visible, erected on the last rocky outcrop. It is a fortress within a fortress, the last refuge that could only be reached by climbing some 60 irregular, slippery steps. The building of these steps alone was an amazing achievement in the Middle

Right
View of the ruins of Peyrepertuse from the air ▶

Following double spread
The Cathar fortress of Quéribus on the craggy slopes of the Pyrenees ▶▶

◀ **Left**
The vaulted Gothic Pillar Hall at Quéribus

Ages – as was the building of these fortresses in these inaccessible places. Peyrepertuse was never attacked. However, after long negotiations Guillaume de Peyrepertuse gave himself up to King Louis IX in 1240.

Quéribus is not as large as Peyrepertuse, but survived longer as a Cathar fortress, perhaps because it was so isolated. It is narrow and tortuous since it reflects the shape of the narrow ridge on which it is built and the walls are pierced with crenels. The Gothic Pillar Room is particularly striking.

The fortress was first mentioned at the beginning of 11th century. It belonged to the counts of Bésalu and was later annexed to the lands of the count of Barcelona becoming the kingdom of Aragón. The Cathar bishop of Razès fled there in 1229 and died in Quéribus in 1241. In the spring of 1255, the fortress was besieged on the order of the French, and in March 1256, Chabert de Barbeia surrendered.

The pure beliefs of the Cathars

The most important religious movement of the Middle Ages first developed in the Rhine region and then spread to southern Europe, in particular to southern France. The Cathars supported purity of mind and asceticism, rejecting all earthly attachments such as marriage, property ownership, the worship of images, relics, saints and war. This undermined basic principles of the Catholic church and medieval society, thus automatically making many enemies. But the Cathar movement also had many followers including the simple country people in the French Midi who felt exploited by the church as well as the aristocracy in Carcassonne, Toulouse and Albi (therefore also known as the Albigenses) who governed their territories independently; they appreciated the independence from Rome offered by the Cathar movement.

The Pope was worried about the loss of influence by the Catholic church, and probably also about the reduction to its income. He called for a crusade against the apostates. In 1209, an army of crusaders stood in front of the gates of Béziers, demanding the surrender of the Cathar inhabitants. Without waiting for the end of the negotiations, Simon de Montfort ordered the entire population of the town slaughtered – between 15,000 and 20,000 people. After this massacre, many surrendered without further fighting, but the Albigensian wars only ended with a treaty in 1229.

A few Cathars were able to escape the crusaders into the rough, inaccessible mountainous region of Corbières, taking refuge in the Cathar fortresses of Peyrepertuse and Quéribus until they too had to surrender after long sieges. The Cathar movement lost much of its influence and by the 14th century it had ceased to exist.

◀ **LEFT**
After a long siege, the fortress of Quéribus, the last refuge of the Cathars, was captured by the troops of the French king

Saumur

Although fortified, the Gothic castle in Saumur is a pleasant construction that undoubtedly contributed the town's epithet "Perle des Anjou". The view from the Loire is especially picturesque, looking towards the other bank, across the old town and up to the towers of the castle standing out in the twilight or floodlit at night.

Situated at the confluence of the Thouet and the Loire, Saumur was always a point of contention, so it was important to build a strong fortress there. It is probable that Fulco Nerra, count of Anjou (987–1040), was the first to build a fortress on the rocky outcrop overlooking the town, but nothing remains of this early fortress. The present castle dates back to Duke Louis of Anjou, the brother of Charles V and of the Duke Jean de Berry. Louis had inherited the castle from his father and rebuilt it in 1340 into a princely residence to match the luxurious palaces of his brothers. It is known exactly what the castle looked like in the past because the famous Book of Hours, or Les très riches Heures du Duc de Berry, produced in 1410 by the Limburg brothers, includes a detailed drawing of the castle on the page for September. The mighty foundations of the feudal fortress of 1230 were incorporated in the new building,

which consisted of four fortified wings built around a courtyard. At the ends are the residential quarters, linked by polygonal towers, built on the round base of the old fortress. The narrow stringcourses on the towers give them a tall, slender appearance.

This impression was further emphasized by the addition, during the time of Duke Louis, of the magnificent roof, so typical of French Gothic: chimneys, turrets with pointed roofs, dormer windows and gilt weathervanes, decorated with the duke's coat of arms rose high up in the sky. This gave the robust, castle-like fortress an elegant, light appearance, just like a fairy tale castle. Unfortunately, many of these features have not survived so the fortified character of the castle of Saumur is much more apparent now than it was in the past.

In the 17th century, the city, which had flourished in the Middle Ages, began to decline and the castle was allowed to fall into disrepair. The northwest wing fell down and was not rebuilt, and the castle was used as a prison in the 17th and 18th centuries. Napoleon turned it into a state prison. Later, between 1830 and 1890, it was used as barracks and arsenal.

Right:
The gate tower. The turrets and bay windows give this fortified castle a light, elegant appearance ▶

Following double spread
View of the castle seen from across the Loire ▶▶

◀ **Left**
A wooden winch in the pump-house of the castle

In 1906 the castle became the property of the city of Saumur and was restored. It now houses two very different museums. The first floor, once the duke's apartments, now contains an arts and craft museum. The collections include tapestries, furniture, paintings and sculptures from the Middle Ages and the Renaissance as well as a collection of faience and porcelain from the Baroque period.

Saumur has traditionally been a center of French equestrianism.The Musée du Cheval (Horse Museum) on the top floor covers everything concerning the horse and its history. The cavalry school was established here in 1768 and Saumur has also been the home of the national riding school since 1972, which includes the famous "Cadre Noir", a French variation on the Spanish riding school in Vienna. The exhibits include saddles, stirrups and bits from many countries as well as pictures relating to horses and riding.

In 2004 a start was made with a thorough renovation of the castle which reopened to public in 2012.

The Loire – a river of nature and culture

The Loire is France's longest and most famous river, 634 miles long. Its source is on Mont Gerbier de Jonc in the southeast of the Massif Central. For about 155 miles, it flows parallel to the river Allier until the latter flows into it. From Nevers, it runs in a wide curve through the Paris basin as far as Orléans and then continues in the direction of Saint-Nazaire where it flows into the Atlantic. Running from south to north, the Loire would appear to be an ideal waterway for France. But there are sandbanks, strong falls and irregular water levels that prevent the effective use of the river as a means of transport. In fact, only small boats use the Loire. After the railway was built in the 19th century, goods were moved by train and the Loire was abandoned completely. Grass, reeds and small bushes invaded the riverbank, which has now become a perfect habitat for wild life such as birds, otters and beavers.

The best-known stretch of the river is the middle section 186 miles long between Gien and Angers. The banks of the Loire and its tributaries are lined with chateaus, fortresses, churches and historic towns that make the region one of the most interesting cultural landscapes in Europe. About one-third of the 300 fortresses and chateaus of the Loire can be visited. They offer a wonderful insight into the life of the French aristocracy and French history.

◀ **LEFT**
Even after the castle was restored in 1904, the collapsed northwest wing was never rebuilt

Versailles

Louis XIV, absolutism and the Baroque are the three concepts that are inseparably associated with the palace at Versailles. Versailles is the climax of French Baroque architecture, often copied but never equalled. In its splendor and its size, it symbolizes the absolute reign and power of Louis XIV, who declared himself the embodiment of the state ("L'état, c'est moi") and was known as the Sun King.

Shortly after Louis XIV (1638–1715) became king at the age of 23, he began building Versailles, the palace that would take 50 years to complete. The new king did not particularly like Paris and the Louvre as a residence, so he chose Versailles instead, although it was not particularly attractive at the time. But this site had no topographical restrictions and he could build what he wanted. Nor would his palace have to compete with beautiful surrounding or other interesting buildings.

Louis XIV inherited the hunting-lodge at Versailles from his father and he set about extending and decorating it. Initially the young king commissioned the architect Louis Le Vau, and when Le Vau died, Louis XIV first hired François d'Orbay, then in 1678, Jules Hardouin-Mansart. He also retained the garden architect André le Nôtre and the painter Charles Le Brun. These three men had already shown their artistic and architectural skills when they built the private castle of Vaux-le-Vicomte, a perfect example of Baroque architecture. It was said that Louis could not accept that any of his subjects should have more sumptuous buildings than himself, which is why he arrested the owner of Vaux-le-Vicomte, Nicolas Fouquet.

Le Vau designed an imposing architectural complex including the palace and park and also an "Ideal Town", situated just in front. Nearly 650 yards long, the facade of the castle consists of a U-shaped central building and two large side wings. The later addition of further forward projecting buildings surrounding the courtyard made the complex over 440 yards deep.

The enormous park behind the chateau, laid out in typical French Baroque style, covers over 12,300 acres. After the Sun King's death Louis XV built the Opera, which was designed by Jacques-Ange Gabriel between 1768 and 1770. From 1682 until the French Revolution in 1789, Versailles was the official residence of the kings of France

RIGHT
The chapel of Versailles, over 82 ft high where mass was celebrated daily ▶

FOLLOWING DOUBLE SPREAD
View of the Royal Courtyard ▶▶

◀ **LEFT**
Entrance gate with gilt decorations. The royal crown conveys a luxuriously symbolic message

– the last one being Louis XVI and his wife Marie Antoinette. In 1837, the chateau of Versailles, abandoned and fallen into disrepair, was turned into a national museum. Today the whole ensemble has been declared a UNESCO world heritage site.

Perhaps the most impressive room inside is the Galerie des Glaces or Hall of Mirrors – 239 ft long, 36 ft wide and 39 ft high. The Hall links the Queen's and the King's Apartments and is embellished with mirrors, gilt decorations and paintings covering the entire ceiling. They depict the most important episodes of the first 17 years of Louis XIV's reign. The Galerie des Glaces is the most visited room in the palace both for its magnificent decorations and its historic atmosphere, having been the scene of many important political events. The Peace of Versailles, signed here in 1783, ended the American Revolutionary War between France, Spain, the United States and Great Britain. In 1870, the November Treaties of Versailles were signed, whereby the South German States joined the North German Alliance. It was here that Kaiser Wilhelm I was declared Emperor of Germany in 1871 and the Versailles treaty ending the Franco-Prussian war was signed in the same year. The French National Assembly met here between 1871 and 1879, and the victorious powers of World War I met in the Hall of Mirrors to sign the Peace of Versailles in 1919. No less magnificent are the adjoining bedrooms of the king and queen, the Grands Appartements and the Galerie des Batailles whose coffered ceiling is decorated with paintings representing France's military history and the busts of outstanding army leaders.

From the terrace in front of the Hall of Mirrors, the gardens of Versailles continue this breathtaking display of magnificence and power. Much work had to be carried out to create this strictly symmetrical garden with pure geometric shapes. Hills had to be levelled, little plantations of trees planted and canals built in order to supply water to the pools, cascades and fountains. Paths and driveways seem to have been drawn with a ruler, thus creating a succession of deliberate, impressive focal points.

Versailles also set the standard for formal Baroque garden design. Louis XIV built the Grand Trianon in the park to the northwest of the main palace, as a pleasure palace. Although it is more modest and smaller than the main building, it was still imposing enough for Napoleon I to reside here in the 18th century. Since World War II it has welcomed important guests of the French state including Richard Nixon in 1969 and Leonid Breshnev in 1971.

The Petit Trianon nearby, with its remarkable wood panelling, was built by Louis XV for his mistress Madame de Pompadour. Because she died before it was completed, he gave it to Madame du Barry of whom he was also very fond. Louis XVI's wife Marie-Antoinette also spent much time there, preferring it to the palace itself.

At her request, Louis XVI built a little village nearby with cottages with thatched roofs and English gardens. It was an idealized representation of country life as painted by Rococo artists. Marie-Antoinette loved to play at being a rustic peasant in this idyllic but unrealistic setting.

◀ LEFT
The State Bedchamber of the Sun King, Louis XIV, who died here on 1 September 1715

FOLLOWING DOUBLE SPREAD
Orangery at the Gardens of Versailles ▶▶

Château de Belœil

The most beautiful castle in Belgium is Belœil, often called the Belgian Versailles. Built as the seat of the de Ligne family, it is about 50 miles southwest of Brussels. It is a fine example of the Belgian interpretation of the French Baroque chateau style.

A long drive lined with beech trees leads to the entrance of Belœil, situated 19 miles to the southeast of Tournai. Claude-Lamoral II de Ligne built the chateau in the 17th century as a moated castle, consisting of a courtyard surrounded by four wings, with a round tower at each of the four corners. Slightly projecting were two lower buildings housing the domestic offices. The whole chateau is reflected in the large moat, forming a magnificent sight. The fountain of Neptune is a copy of one at Versailles.

The gardens too were laid out in the formal French style with flower borders, statues of gods, fountains and standard roses. Maréchal Charles-Joseph de Ligne, the son of Claude-Lamoral, expressed his thoughts on his country and his home as follows: "A man has two fatherlands: his own and France." With this statement he showed himself a true prince of Rococo and with the help of the Paris architect François-Joseph Bélanger, he converted the gardens into an English-style park.

The interior of the chateau is decorated with Gobelin tapestries, paintings and fine antique furniture. In one of the towers is a rather macabre curiosity: preserved in a little gold pouch are locks of hair belonging to Marie-Antoinette, the French queen beheaded in 1793. In the gardens is Belœil Minibel, which contains miniature models of interesting places and buildings of Belgium such as the Hôtel de Ville and the Grand Palais from Brussels, the belltower from Bruges, the Coo waterfalls and many others.

RIGHT
The four-sided castle building is reflected in the large moat ▶

FOLLOWING DOUBLE SPREAD
This part of the Chateau de Belœil is reminiscent of a "baby Versailles" ▶▶

Château de Bouillon

The chateau of the crusader Godfrey of Bouillon dominates the little town on the bank of the river Semois, situated in the middle of the Ardennes near the French border. It is the most important medieval fortresses with one of the oldest meeting halls in Belgium.

Because of it strategically favorable location, the chateau of Bouillon, first mentioned in 988, became a bone of contention among the rulers of the region and played an increasingly important role in the conflicts between France and the Habsburgs. The fortress was besieged at least seventeen times. The improvement in weapons, and the invention of firearms and new military war strategies demanded a constant adaptation of its defensive structure. The castle was gradually converted into a fortress and the famous French fortress architect Vauban rebuilt it in 1680, equipping it with the latest defense features to meet the new demands of warfare, which explains why there is very little left of the original medieval fortifications. The present appearance of the fortress dates from the 17th to the 19th century.

Behind the first bridge are the ruins of the old outer fort. The top part and two of the four towers were demolished so that the area could be converted into a battery.

This was the only way of effectively installing heavy defenses against artillery. The flanking towers behind the second bridge suffered a similar fate: the top part was also removed to make room for the battery. A third drawbridge over the old moat gave access to the inner fortress. Behind walls several yards thick, dating from the 11th and 12th century, is the "salle primitive" or primitive hall, one of the oldest assembly halls in Belgium. From the Austrian to wer, there is a magnificent view of the whole 1,100 ft fortress complex and the surrounding valleys.

RIGHT
The residential quarters of the castle are functional rather than luxurious ▶

FOLLOWING DOUBLE SPREAD
The fortress rises impressively above the rolling hills of the Ardennes ▶▶

◀ **LEFT**
Prisoners were kept in the windowless dungeon and fed on bread and water

Het Loo, Apeldoorn

Apeldoorn on the east of National Park the Veluwe is a city of delightful villas and gardens. The palace of Het Loo with its famous formal gardens, north of the city, undoubtedly contributed to this reputation because it was the Dutch royal family's summer residence from the time it was first built until 1975.

No one in the late 17th century would have anticipated the grandiose development of this site in the heart of the Netherlands. On the contrary, contemporaries shook their heads in disbelief when the king-governor, Willem III, decided to move here. His passion for hunting was well known, but this did not seem a good enough reason to move to this area – then known only for being inhospitable. But Willem III liked the extensive hunting grounds near Apeldoorn so much that he decided to build a pleasure palace there for himself and his wife Mary Stuart. Designed by the architects Jacob Roman and Daniel Marot, it was built between 1685 and 1692.

Marot designed many buildings, mainly in The Hague and also elsewhere in the Netherlands. For the king, the two men designed a Baroque palace, inspired by Versailles (see page 192). It was rebuilt during the reign of King Louis Napoleon, and later also by Queen Wilhelmina. The pleasantly restrained exterior contrasts strongly with the magnificently sumptuous interior. After the Dutch royal family moved out in 1975, the buildings were comprehensively restored. Since 1984, the palace has been the "Rijksmuseum Paleis Het Loo" and is open to the public. The three centuries of the royal house of Orange-Nassau are illustrated by historical documents, medals, paintings, antique furniture, royal garments, valuable ceramics and precious china. Further attractions are the riding-stable with its ornate carriages, sledges and Queen Wilhelmina's painting carriage. She would be driven in it through the countryside to picturesque locations where she could indulge her hobby of painting landscapes. The Baroque parterres in the garden of Het Loo were also designed by Marot and are particularly beautiful in spring and summer. Every year they are arranged as they were in the 17th century, and the fountains and other water works still play as they did in the past. Together with the numerous stone statues, vases and pergolas, they create a spectacular impression that is a pleasing distraction from the hustle and bustle of Europe in the 21st century.

RIGHT
The Dutch royal family dined here in summer until 1975 ▶

FOLLOWING DOUBLE SPREAD
Willem III decided to build the palace of Het Loo in the rather inhospitable countryside near Apeldoorn because he thought it was ideal for hunting ▶

NEXT DOUBLE SPREAD
The state drawing room ▶▶▶

◀ **LEFT**
The baroque gardens contain many fountains and cascades such as this fountain of Venus surrounded by gilded swans

BINNENHOF

Thousands of people line the streets and form a guard of honour along the route of the golden carriage, as it carries the Queen of the Netherlands from Noordeinde Palace to the Binnenhof to read the Queen's Speech. This is not a description of an occasion from the distant past but an event that still takes place annually when the Dutch parliament opens for "Prinsjesdag" – the third Tuesday of Sep-tember. It is a day of celebration for all supporters of the monarchy and the house of Orange.

The Binnenhof is a medieval castle that has been involved in the fate of The Hague from its earliest beginnings. The Hague, officially known as Gravenhage, is a modern, cosmopolitan, residential city that is also the seat of government and home of the ministries, communications, administration, the international Court of Justice and Academy of International Law. It is also a cultural center with some outstanding modern architecture. The Binnenhof, a red-brown brick building in the center of the old town, is still the center of the political world. "Binnenhof" is the Dutch word for "inner bailey", but in this context it describes the country's center of government.

In 1247, Willem II, Count of Holland and German king (1247–56), built a hunting lodge here in the style of a castle. His son Floris V established his residence here and enlarged it by adding the Ridderzaal, the Knight's Hall, which is still the center of the Binnenhof. These buildings form the core of the palace complex, which is arranged around two courtyards.

Although a new extension was added to the Binnenhof in 1992 to house the parliament and the building has experienced many changes in the course of its long history, it has always preserved its identity as symbol of Dutch democracy. On the east side of the courtyard is the Ridderzaal building that was erected on 13th century foundations. The Ridderzaal has been occupied by the governors since the time of Moritz of Nassau-Orange (1585). The governors had their own entrance made, the Stadhouderspoort, built in Renaissance style. Until 1786, this could be used only by them.

The rectangular building is demarcated by four corner towers. The Ridderzaal was originally planned as a Gothic-style banqueting hall by Gerard van Leyden in the 13th century. The trussed roof with its 59 ft wooden beams is quite remarkable.

The Dutch city's coat-of-arms is displayed and there is a rose window with the most important Dutch ruling dynasties. The Ridderzaal is 131 ft long and 66 ft wide, and has been used for a variety of purposes throughout its history. It was renovated at the beginning of the 20th century and since then has been used as a venue for ceremonial occasions, such as the opening of parliament. The northwest facades of the surrounding buildings overlooking a lake were built in the 17th century. These buildings used to house the chambers of the Dutch

RIGHT
The Ridderzaal in the Binnenhof is still an important official center of Dutch politics ▶

parliament until it moved to the new extension. Before they became the seat of parliament in 1815, they were used in turn as the venue for the first national assembly, as a residence by Napoleon's brother Louis Napoleon, and then as a hospital. The architect Daniel Marot, who designed many buildings in The Hague, also designed the sumptuous Trèveszaal, named after the Trèves Peace Treaty.

The Grenadierspoort is the other entrance to the palace complex. On the left of this gate is the Torentje, an octagonal tower that houses the headquarters of the Prime Minister of the Netherlands.

When Queen Beatrix of the Netherlands makes her way to the Binnenhof in her golden coach to read the Queen's speech, she sets off from the Royal Palace. This is not the queen's residence, but her official headquarters and the ceremonial venue for state receptions. (The royal family lives in the Paleis Huis ten Bosch, a little way from the town center.) The core of the palace dates from 1553 and in 1640, the architects Pieter Post and Jacob van Campen rebuilt it in the French style for Frederik Hendrik's mother. They created a classical building, consisting of a long central section flanked by two lateral wings that enclose a main courtyard. The projecting central part of the two-storied building draws the eye towards the porch, flanked by pillars with three French windows above and embellished with stone garlands. These open onto a balcony with a balustrade used by the monarch to acknowledge and greet the subjects. A triangular gable decorated with reliefs breaks up the roofline above the projecting central part. The garden of the royal palace is now open to the public.

Extensive renovation works on the Binnenhof will commence in 2020 and will last until mid-2025.

◀ **LEFT**
The buildings around the Ridderzaal date from the 17th century and house the chambers of the Dutch parliament

The Mauritshuis

Immediately behind the Binnenhof is the Mauritshuis, overlooking a small lake. The Mauritshius was built between 1633 and 1644 for Count Johann Maurits von Nassau, governor of Brazil. It was built in strict classical style with pilasters and a triangular gable that emphasises the verticality of the facade.

One of the most beautiful museums in The Hague, it now houses the remarkable Royal Paintings collection. The lavishly restored rooms provide the perfect setting for these Old Dutch Masters ranging from the 17th to the 19th century. The collection includes paintings by Rembrandt, Jan Vermeer, Rubens, Jacob Ruisdael, Brueghel and Rogier van der Weyden.

BLENHEIM PALACE

Blenheim Palace, situated some 8 miles north of Oxford, was given to the Duke of Marlborough by Queen Anne in recognition of services rendered to the nation. This magnificent English Baroque palace is set in a splendid park, considered one of the high points of English landscape gardening.

On 13 August 1704, an event took place that drastically changed the balance of power in Europe and restored Britain's self-confidence in itself as a world power. The Allies, led by the Duke of Marlborough and Prince Eugéne of Austria, won their first great victory in the War of the Spanish Succession. They defeated the armies of Louis XIV in the battle of Höchstädt and Blindheim (Blenheim in English) on the Danube, thereby showing that the Sun King could be defeated. This victory was the beginning of the end of French domination in Europe.

Queen Anne granted the Woodstock estate as a fief to John Churchill, Duke of Marlborough (1650–1722) and the British Parliament awarded him £240,000, then an immense sum, to build himself a palace worthy of his victory. Named after the site of the battle, Blenheim Palace was a large, imposing construction, designed with a style and impressiveness appropriate to a gift from the nation made in recognition of Marlborough's services to his country; its residential function was only secondary.

John Vanbrugh (1664–1726) was an obvious choice as architect because he had already made a name for himself with Castle Howard (see page 232). He worked on Blenheim with Nicolas Hawksmoor (1661–1736), who had also worked with him on Castle Howard and who had become famous for his Baroque churches in London. These two architects are today considered the most important representatives of the English Baroque style, and they built Blenheim Palace together between 1705 and 1725.

Like many Renaissance palaces, Blenheim Palace has four corner pavilions linked by galleries. The massive appearance of the square pavilions is reminiscent of the watchtowers in old fortresses.

The open arcades give an elegant effect and the continuation of the rhythmically structured facade linking the pavilions with the residential quarters creates a harmonious unity. The side facades have tall arched windows, cornices and semi-circular central projecting structures.

An imposing colonnaded portal with a triangular pediment above the entrance, flanked by semi-cir-

RIGHT
The entrance portal of the north facade has imposing banded columns ▶

FOLLOWING DOUBLE SPREAD
The west front of Blenheim Palace ▶▶

◀ **LEFT**
Sphinx statue

cular, curved facades, emphasizes the main central building as the focal point of the castle. Adjoining it are the two side wings that house the stables and domestic offices. These buildings each have an interior courtyard at the back while their magnificent facades at the front overlook the main courtyard of the palace.

This main courtyard is bounded on the fourth side – the entrance side – by a colonnaded gallery. Like the corner pavilions, the arrangement of a closed courtyard almost completely surrounded by buildings is more reminiscent of a fortified castle than of French Baroque palaces. Like many other Baroque palaces, Blenheim Palace was inspired by Versailles. Here however, the architects adapted the design to English requirements, thereby creating their own style that had a more robust and theatrical effect than the French Baroque.

The interior is equally impressive. The imposing entrance hall is 66 ft high, and decorated with ceiling paintings and tapestries representing scenes from the Duke of Marlborough's victorious battles. The duke was also a successful diplomat and politician. Throughout the building, exquisite furniture, family portraits, precious silver and rare porcelain reflect the sophisticated taste of the Churchill family. The dynamic and legendary British Prime Minister, Winston Churchill, was born here in 1874.

Vanbrugh created a formal garden in the French style befitting the Baroque style of the castle, with flowerbeds, straight paths leading to the castle, fountains and a canal. The famous garden designer Lancelot "Capability" Brown did away with these gardens and turned them into a landscaped park. Everything was carefully planted and positioned to create a beautiful interplay of various shades of green, while producing a very natural effect.

Today, Blenheim Palace also has a French terraced garden next to the house, laid out between 1925 and 1930. It is set in a park of 2,100 acres with wild animals, a nature trail, footpaths and a lake made from the former canal. A triumphal arch and victory columns surrounded by groups of trees representing the positions of the armies in the battle of Blenheim are reminders of the great victory of 1704 that was the origin of the palace.

To mark 100 years since the birth of Brown, 2016 saw celebrations happening throughout the year.

◀ **LEFT**
The Column of Victory, topped with a statue of the first Duke of Marlborough, overlooks the Park from a height of 134.5 ft

"Capability" Brown, the most famous landscape gardener

The first English landscaped garden was an expression of the new emerging liberalism which opposed French absolutism, symbolized by the rigidity of the formal Baroque garden. The most famous of all landscape gardeners was Lancelot "Capability" Brown who acquired his unusual nickname because when asked by a prospective client for his opinion of a site, he always replied that their park had great "capabilities".

Hampton Court Palace

The palace of Hampton Court, situated close to London, was the residence of the English monarchs between the 16th and 19th century. Its fascination lies in its captivating combination of Tudor and French Baroque styles.

When Cardinal Thomas Wolsey built Hampton Court on the banks of the Thames, 14 miles southwest of London, it was considered the most splendid palace in the country. It had everything that a castle should have: towers, chimneys and battlements. The palace was built between 1515 and 1525 in the Tudor style. This style was the last phase of perpendicular Gothic – the name given to the late English Gothic characterized by its emphasis on verticality and grid-like arrangement of walls and windows.

Wolsey did not enjoy Hampton Court for very long because he gave it to Henry VIII a year after it was finished (1526). The Cardinal had fallen from grace and hoped to regain the king's favor in this way. But his efforts were in vain: Wolsey was removed from office four years later.

Nevertheless, Wolsey had made the king very happy. Henry VIII loved Hampton Court so much that he made it his main residence and lived there with his wife, Anne Boleyn, changing and enlarging the building. In 1540, he rebuilt the second interior courtyard, which became the Clock Court when Nicholas Oursian was commissioned to produce an astronomical clock for it. The clock can still be seen working today. The library and the Great Hall with its wonderful hammer beam roof were also built under Henry VIII, and he enlarged the garden.

Elizabeth I, the daughter of Henry VIII, and Anne Boleyn, also preferred Hampton Court as a residence. It was at Hampton Court that she received the news of the victory of the English fleet over the Spanish Armada. Elizabeth was very interested in gardening and collected exotic plants from all over the world, brought back for her by explorers such as Francis Drake and Walter Raleigh.

The arrival of William of Orange and his wife Mary Stuart marked the beginning of a new era for Hampton Court. After only a year in power, they pulled down parts of the old Tudor castle and rebuilt it. The royal architect Christopher Wren was commissioned to create another "Versailles" because they did not want to live in the medieval castle of Whitehall. Wren's original plans were probably more inspired by the Louvre, and they were only carried out in part, a fact that explains the fascinating mixture of styles. However, to describe Hampton Court as the English Versailles would be a slight exaggeration.

The east and south wing were rebuilt. The shell of the building was completed during William's lifetime, but the interior with the sumptuous State Apartments was not yet finished

Right
Baroque bed at state bedchamber ▶

Following double spread
Overall view of the south-facade with its rich relief. The French influence is seen in the arrangement of the many windows ▶▶

at the time of this death. The result is a four-storied building with a semi-basement, a main floor and two mezzanine floors. The contrast between the bright red bricks and the dressed Portland stone is particularly attractive in the facade, which is embellished with ornate details and has a projecting stone section with decorative reliefs. The French influence is also apparent in the large number of windows, which differ in shape on each floor.

The gardens in front of the two wings slope down to the River Thames. The south wing overlooks the smaller and more intimate "Privy Garden", while the main garden extends in front of the east wing. Daniel Marot designed the parterre. Like the palace itself, the park and gardens have changed in the course of time to reflect the taste of the inhabitants, so they combine several styles. Some parts are still in Tudor style, others are in the formal geometric Baroque style, while yet other areas are more like wild gardens. The famous Hampton Court maze formed of tall yew hedges was created in the time of William and Mary.

The last monarch to reside in Hampton Court was George III (1683–1760). In 1839, the castle and gardens were opened to the public and they remain so to this day.

In 2015, Hampton Court brought all 500 years of history to life with a series of celebrations. Building at the palace began on 12 February 1515.

Christopher Wren, royal architect

Christopher Wren was born in 1632. He first studied natural sciences, after which he became a professor of astronomy. It was only in 1663 that he began working as an architect. The chapel at Pembroke College, Cambridge was built according to his designs and he was also a member of the Committee for the Restoration of the old St Paul's Cathedral. Two years later, he spent nine months in Paris where he met Bernini and FranŹois Mansart and saw their plans for the Louvre as well as many other famous churches. This visit was to influence him for the rest of his life. Soon after, he had an amazing stroke of luck as an architect. In September 1666, the City of London was partially destroyed by the Great Fire of London and 13,000 houses and 87 churches burnt down. Upon his return from Paris, Wren drew up a plan for the reconstruction of London. It was rejected but it had a great influence on the rebuilding work in which he was deeply involved. Wren built 51 new churches (15 have survived), including the new St Paul's Cathedral, his masterpiece. As far as secular architecture is concerned, apart from his work at Hampton Court, he built only a few houses, but played an important part in the development of English architecture. Christopher Wren died in Hampton Court in 1723.

◀ **LEFT**
The West front and main entrance of Hampton Court Palace

FOLLOWING DOUBLE SPREAD
View on Hampton Court gardens ▶▶

CASTLE HOWARD

Castle Howard is recognized as one of the greatest achievements of Baroque architecture in England. When Horace Walpole visited it in 1772 he wrote: "Nobody... had informed me that I should at one view see a palace, a town, a fortified city, temples on high places, woods worthy of being each a metropolis of the Druids, vales connected to hills by other woods, the noblest lawn in the world, fenced by half the horizon, and a mausoleum that would tempt one to be buried alive; in short I have seen gigantic places before, but never a sublime one."

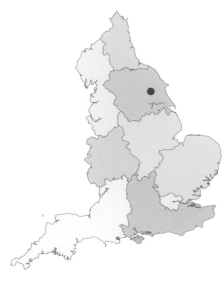

The impressive family seat of the Howards is a celebrated stately home situated some 15 miles to the north-east of York in northern England. It was built by Charles Howard, the third Earl of Carlisle, who had only one ambition when he built it: he wanted to surpass and impress his fellow countrymen, creating a symbol that would represent the wealth and pride of aristocratic landowners. There is no doubt that he was sucessful.

In 1699, Charles Howard commissioned John Vanbrugh to draw up plans for a castle. Vanbrugh was a self-taught architect, yet he produced the architectural masterpiece of Castle Howard, a feat that made him one of the most sought-after architects in England. He sought the help of the brilliant architect Nicholas Hawksmoor, a pupil of the royal court architect Christopher Wren, to help him in drawing up the detailed plans and supervising the work between 1700 and 1726. Nicholas Hawksmoor took over the project after Vanbrugh's death.

Before his career as an architect, Vanbrugh led a turbulent life as a soldier, a spy in France and a playwright. He drew up plans for an imposing, magnificent, theatrical palace with a 65 ft gallery, and an extravagant 82 ft entrance hall, the focal point and center of the castle building. This hall is surmounted by a spectacular dome and flanked by stairwells that can be seen through open arches. The facades are embellished with a wealth of decorative features and friezes depicting seahorses and cherubs. The roundarched windows are framed by Doric pilasters on the north facades, and Corinthian pilasters on the south facade. The north facade is further decorated with statues and vases in niches in the wall, while the roof balustrade is ornamented with sculptures and completes the building in a dramatic manner.

RIGHT
The quintessence of wealth and power: Castle Howard with its dome above the 82 ft high entrance hall. In the foreground is the Atlas fountain ▶

FOLLOWING DOUBLE SPREAD
View of the south front ▶▶

◀ **Links**
Figure of Hercules

Castle Howard had no official or ceremonial function, so its interior is not as imposing or consistent as that of other Baroque buildings, such as the palaces of Germany or Austria. Various collections are on display, assembled by members of the family over the course of the past three centuries. The collection of paintings is particularly remarkable, including works by English and Italian masters such as Canaletto, Rubens, Raphael, John Jackson and Hans Holbein. There is also an interesting collection of fine china with some 300 exhibits, including Chinese, Meissen and Chelsea porcelain.

The 10,000 acre garden and park surrounding Castle Howard are very famous. The large lake with the building in the background is probably one of the most photographed views. Rose enthusiasts will find the rose garden absolutely irresistible as old and new roses exude their heady, captivating fragrance throughout the summer.

Another delightful garden is Ray Wood, which combines artistic gardening and botanical science. The garden contains one of the largest private plant collections in Europe, with about 800 species and varieties of rhododendron that turn this part of the park into a sea of color in the summer.

The magnificent park with its remarkable follies and monuments symbolizes the pride of the aristocracy, including an obelisk, a gatehouse and fortifications – every walk provides new surprises and beautiful perspectives. The large pyramid, built by Hawksmoor in 1728, was erected in honor of the founder of the Carlisle family. The Temple of the Four Winds (1725–28), a cube-shaped construction surmounted by a cupola, is reminiscent of Palladio's Villa Rotonda in Vicenza.

Known originally as the Temple of Diana, it takes its present name from the fact that the porticos on each of the four facades open up to the four cardinal points of the compass.

The Mausoleum

The largest monument in the park is the Mausoleum, which the Earl helped design. The correspondence between him and his architect Nicholas Hawksmoor reflects their exchange of ideas before the building started. Hawksmoor built it between 1729 and 1744. It is a rotunda, erected on a plinth, surrounded by a colonnade of Doric columns. This is where Charles Howard, the third Earl of Carlisle, was buried when the mausoleum was completed. This was in fulfilment of his last wish, expressed in his will, which stipulated that he should buried in the mausoleum near his home. The mausoleum is the private resting place of many members of the Howard family.

KENSINGTON PALACE

William III, Mary Stuart, George II, Queen Victoria, Princess Margaret, Prince Charles and Princess Diana are but a few of the famous names that are closely connected with Kensington Palace. It was used for a while as a town residence by some English kings, but later became the residence of other members of the royal family.

Kensington Palace was built after the Glorious Revolution in 1689, when William III of Orange and his wife Mary Stuart came to power. Because they did not particularly like the medieval palace of Whitehall, they built or extended other palaces such as Hampton Court Palace (see page 224) and Kensington Palace. The king bought Nottingham House in Kensington from his minister, the Earl of Nottingham, and asked the court architect Christopher Wren to convert it into a palace appropriate to their position.

Wren added the solid, brick manor house with stables and domestic offices, a chapel and several apartments for the royal couple. The new facade with a projecting central section and pilasters create a strong vertical impression. However, it is quite restrained for a royal palace and even the roof balustrade over the central projection, decorated with urns, does not hide the fact that Kensington Palace was originally "only" a manor house. Perhaps it was this rather plain, unassuming appearance of the building that the royal couple appreciated because it did not immediately evoke images of court life and government.

George I wanted something larger and more sumptuous. In the 1820s, he asked William Kent and Colin Campbell, who were both champions of the Palladian style, to alter and extend the existing building. They added several state rooms and enlarged Kensington Palace in such a way that all the buildings were grouped around three internal courtyards.

The last monarch to live in Kensington Palace was George II. Since then it has been inhabited by other members of the royal family. Traditionally, the west wing has been inhabited by the successor to the throne, the Prince of Wales and his family. This changed in the late 20th century when Prince Charles and Princess Diana separated in 1992 and Prince Charles moved into Lancaster House.

Kensington Palace is now inhabited by several minor members of the royal family, including Duke and Duchess of Kent, the Duke and Duchess of Gloucester, the Earl of Ulster, Lady Davina Windsor and Lady Rose Windsor. The State Apartments on the top floor of the Palace are particularly interesting because they were designed in different styles by famous English architects, including

RIGHT
Until they separated Prince Charles and Princess Diana lived in Kensington Palace ▶

◀ **Links**
Painted ceiling inside Kensington Palace

Christopher Wren, William Kent and Nicholas Hawksmoor, who also built the orangery to the north of the palace in 1704. While the rooms designed by Wren are imposing and formal with dark panelled walls, those designed by Kent appear more luxurious and lavish. William Kent had spent a long time in Rome and was influenced by late Italian Baroque architecture. He was one of the most versatile English architects and demonstrated this at Kensington Palace: while he designed the King's Staircase in the style of Venetian Baroque with trompe l'oeil wall paintings, he decorated the Cupola Room in neoclassical style with a coffered ceiling, large pilasters, statues in wall niches and a chimney flanked by double columns, anticipating the architectural style of 18th century. The wall paintings with arabesques in the Presence Chamber are reminiscent of the works of Renaissance artists such as Raphael. Wren's Queen's Staircase is decorated with magnificent wrought-iron work by Tijou, and leads to the Queen's gallery. The oak wood panels and woodcarvings by Grinling Gibbons are the perfect setting for the portraits of English rulers. Wren decorated the King's Gallery with dark green wallpaper and a painted wooden ceiling. On the orders of William III a large wind dial was installed in the gallery, which still indicates in which direction the wind is blowing. Time seems to have stood still in the royal private apartments, which are still furnished as if the occupants are about to return at any moment. Even the dolls and toys belonging to Queen Victoria, who was born in Kensington Palace, are still there. On the ground floor is a display of aristocratic gowns and clothes that date from 1750 until the present day, including Princess Diana's wedding gown. Kensington Gardens are to the east of Kensington Palace. Originally, they were created as a private garden for the royal family. Queen Caroline, George II's wife, was responsible for the garden's present appearance, with the sunken ornamental garden near the palace. Today Kensington Gardens are joined to Hyde Park, thus forming the largest park in London. Queen Victoria erected the Albert Memorial on the southern edge of Kensington Gardens in honour of her husband Prince Albert. Today, prince William and Kate live in Apartment 1A at Kensington Palace.

The Albert Memorial

Prince Albert of Saxe-Coburg, husband of Queen Victoria, died from typhoid fever in 1861 at the age of 42. The bronze statue of Albert the Prince Consort holding the catalogue of the Great Exhibition of 1851, which he had initiated, rests on a plinth beneath a richly decorated neo-Gothic baldachin nearly 200 ft high. The pedestal is adorned with 178 sculptures of famous artists and scientists.

◀ **LEFT**
Statue of Queen Victoria situated outside Kensington Palace

Longleat House

The rolling hills of Wiltshire in southern England are covered with green fields and woodland. At the heart of this peaceful, agricultural landscape is Longleat, a perfect example of Elizabethan Renaissance architecture and also a pioneer in opening stately homes to the public.

Longleat is built on the site of an ancient Augustine monastery that was bought by Sir John Thynne in 1540 for 53 pounds after the monastery was dissolved. He commissioned Robert Smythson, the best architect of the time, to design and build a castle befitting his social standing. The building was erected between 1572 and 1580 using brick, which was the popular building material at the time. It was readily available and because of the small size of each brick, it could be used to create ornamental features. Smythson was clearly inspired by the Renaissance palazzos of Northern Italy and designed a very compact, but magnificently composed, structure of fine proportions.

The three-storied building has a rectangular ground plan with two interior courtyards. From the outside, the middle floor is immediately identifiable as the main one because of its tall windows. The strict symmetry of the facade was new at the time. The short sides of the rectangle are decorated with projecting bays at the center (with two doors) and each end. In contrast, the longer facades have two projecting bays in the center as well as similar ones at each end. All these bays are two windows wide. The center of the long entrance front has a handsome main porch with an elegant flight of steps. It is flanked by columns and surmounted by a triangular pediment.

The cornices running between the floors along the entire facade link the projecting bays with the rest of the facade. The emphasis on these horizontal features seems to link the house to the earth, anchoring it firmly. The tall windows with their mullions and the pilasters on the projecting bays counteract this horizontal effect. Following the Italian example, the pilasters framing the windows are Doric on the ground floor, then Ionic, then Corinthian. The roof reflects the two opposing horizontal and vertical forces and combines them. A balustrade runs along the whole roof, completing the horizontal effect at the top of the building, while the sculptures on the balustrade and the numerous tall chimneys seem to create a link with the sky. While the exterior appearance of Longleat has remained mostly unchanged throughout the centuries, the interior has undergone many alterations. This is often the case in old houses and castles, which are constantly renewed and altered by the inhabitants to reflect their taste and to meet contemporary standards of comfort. Only the hall with the hammer beam ceiling has survived from the original Elizabethan building. The rest has been altered and redecorated, particularly in the 19th century.

RIGHT
The gates of Longleat are always open to visitors ▶

FOLLOWING DOUBLE SPREAD
The strict symmetry of the facade is a fine example of Elizabethan Renaissance architecture ▶▶

The rooms open to the public have wonderful coffered ceilings, Gobelin tapestries, velvet and leather wall hangings and paintings by artists such as Tintoretto and Ruisdael.

Alexander Thynne, the seventh Marquess of Bath, a direct descendant of Sir John Thynne who built the house and the present owner of Longleat, has decorated his private apartments according to his own very personal taste. A true eccentric and individualist, he paints and is writing a multi-volume autobiography. "Keyhole glimpses into my psyche" is the title of a series of colorful, burlesque wall paintings that also decorate the dining room and nursery. He decorated the guestroom, called the Kama Sutra room, with scenes from the book of the same name as well as a gallery showing his lovers (whom he calls his "wifelets") in chronological order.

The present marquess has unconventional ideas reflected in the management of his estate. People visiting Longleat out of architectural or artistic interest may be surprised on arrival by the wild animals roaming in the park. Lions, elephants, zebras and giraffes graze on this not-so-perfect English lawn, and tigers are a particular attraction. Longleat has the oldest safari park in Britain, opened by the previous marquess in 1966 (The Times newspaper warned against visiting Longleat) in order to help finance his expensive property. His sons have been as adventurous as their father and the leisure enterprises at Longleat have been considerably enlarged, with a holiday village, a leisure park and other attractions. In addition, Lord Bath has created several mazes including the world's longest hedge maze. Some of these are very difficult, reflecting his slogan "Go to Longleat to get lost".

Longleat, a pioneer of tourism

When the sixth Marquis of Bath inherited Longleat, he also inherited an estate duty bill of several million pounds. Because he did not want to sell the property, he opened the castle to the general public in 1948, charging a reasonable entrance fee. Longleat was the first large British country estate to open its doors to visitors on this scale. Today over 700 historic houses are open to the public.

◀ **LEFT**
View of Longleat
and its safari park

MONTACUTE HOUSE

The British are prone to understatement. But even so, to describe this wonderfully beautiful Elizabethan country estate merely as a house or a manor house is an understatement indeed, and by no means does it justice. It is not without reason that Montacute was chosen as the setting for the award-winning film "Sense and Sensibility".

The whole of the picturesque little village of Montacute near Yeovil in the county of Somerset is classified as a national monument. The houses built from honey-colored stone glow warmly in the sun because they, like Montacute House nearby, are built from Ham Hill stone, also known as Hamstone. This local limestone, typical of the region, was quarried from neighboring Ham Hill. The village and house take their name from a steep local hill known as St Michael Mount, described in Latin as mons acutus meaning "pointed hill". At the top of the hill is a lookout tower with a panoramic view of the village and Montacute House.

The house was built by Edward Phelips at the end of the 16th century and was completed in 1599. The successful lawyer, who became Speaker in the House of Commons under James I, was one of those rising aristocrats in England who wanted a residence befitting his social standing. They wanted appropriate surroundings where they could entertain members of the government, or even the Queen with her court. Many of these so-called Prodigy Houses were built between 1570 and 1620.

Montacute House is distinguished by the simple elegance of its sober facade. It is built on an H-shaped ground plan, with a long main building and very short side wings projecting to the front and back. The house is embellished with Flemishstyle gables.

In the center of the facade is a projecting structure framed by pilasters, which emphasises the entrance area. The large porch is embellished with archivolts, the arches in the reveals of walls that were especially common in Romanesque and Gothic churches. Over the entrance is a coat-of-arms, a typical decorative element in Tudor architecture. Above is a decorative frieze that counterbalances the fluted pilasters.

The large windows with vertical mullions are reminiscent of perpendicular Gothic – as late Gothic is called in England – with its distinctive emphasis on the vertical. They divide up the facade, but they are not as numerous as at Hardwick, or Wollaton Hall, buildings described as having "more glass than wall". The windows are framed by fluted pilasters, placing the emphasis again on the vertical, counterbalanced visually by the horizontal cornices, friezes and balustrade.

The rigorous effect of this structure is lightened by the figures that adorn the top floor, standing on twisted columns. They represent nine heroes wearing Roman armor: Godfrey of Bouillon, Charles the Great, King Arthur, Caesar, Alexander the Great, Hector, Judas Mac-

RIGHT
Summerhouse in East Court, Montacute House ▶

FOLLOWING DOUBLE SPREAD
The south view of the house reveals Flemish influence in the shaped gables ▶▶

cabaeus, David and Joshua. The roof itself, with its numerous, pillar-shaped chimneys, is ornamented with a stone balustrade that runs all round, interrupted by the many gables. The house is strongly symmetrical with a successful interaction between the vertical and horizontal elements.

The garden reflects the symmetry of the house. Near the house, it is formal with flowerbeds and old roses. Straight paths lined with cone-shaped topiary and balustrades with obelisks carry the stylistic elements of the house into the garden. Two decorative two-storied pavilions at the corners of the forecourt have no other function than to bring optical harmony between the house and its surroundings, thus creating a beautiful transition between the outside and the inside. The whole is surrounded by a landscaped park.

The pleasant interior of Montacute House is furnished with valuable 17th and 18th century pieces. The walls are decorated with exquisite wallpaper, fabrics and paintings. Because there is no electricity in the rooms, on rainy days their beauty is concealed in the dark. The house also includes a long gallery, one of the largest of its kind in England, with over a hundred Elizabethan and Jacobean portraits, on long-term loan from the National Portrait Gallery.

Barrington Court

Just a few miles from Montacute House is Barrington Court, a Tudor-style manor house. It was probably built in 1530, and still exudes a medieval atmosphere. It is built on a symmetrical, U-shaped ground plan with a staircase tower in a corner of the courtyard. The formal garden, influenced by Gertrude Jekyll, has a series of "rooms" separated by stone walls, such as the white garden, the rose garden, the lily garden and the kitchen garden.

◀ **LEFT**
Wibbly, wobbly hedge
at Montacute House

STRAWBERRY HILL

A massive, round tower with battlements, an elegant slender tower with a coneshaped roof, massive stonework and pointed arched windows: Strawberry Hill has everything a medieval English castle should have – yet it is not a medieval castle! Strawberry Hill in its present form was built in the mid-18th century and played an important role in the Gothic Revival in England.

Strawberry Hill, overlooking the River Thames, is situated in Twickenham southwest of London. Like Chiswick, Richmond and Kew, it was a popular location with the upper classes during the Georgian period. At the beginning of the 18th century, many prosperous Londoners had a villa, manor house or country estate in the rolling countryside around Twickenham. One such was Horace Walpole (1717–97). The English writer was the son of the Prime Minister Sir Robert Walpole, and after studying at Eton and Cambridge, he traveled through Italy and France with the English poet, Thomas Gray. In 1741, he became a member of the House of Commons. Six years later, in the spring of 1747, Walpole rented Strawberry Hill, built in 1698. A year later, he decided to buy the property and subsequently rebuilt it completely. It was not rebuilt according to the plans of an architect, but to those of the client, as was often the custom in Georgian times. These self-appointed architects were sometimes disdainfully described as "dilettantes". But Walpole was not the only dilettante who took part in drawing up the plans for his new house; he had founded a "committee of taste" consisting of friends who contributed ideas and suggestions.

During the following twenty years, the villa was gradually turned into a small Gothic Revival castle that was ten times as big as the original building. The various parts of the building fulfilled all the functions they would have done in a castle: a large gallery, an entrance hall with an imposing staircase, a large state-room for official receptions, a Chinese cabinet, a breakfast room, several bedrooms, and cellars for wine and beer. The castle replicated the structure of castles of the past with the domestic offices on the ground floor, the state rooms and banqueting hall on the first floor and the bedrooms on the second floor. The organically structured complex also included a chapel in the woods, a printing-house and a cottage in the garden.

However, the number of buildings and functions shows that Strawberry Hill had very little in common with a real medieval castle. It actually shows that Walpole was inspired by the romantic idea of the medieval castle, as were many others in Europe during that period. Indeed, this romantic, idealized concept of the medieval castle that influenced European castle architecture during the 18th and 19th century resulted in a number of historically imaginative fairy tale castles such as Burg Lichtenstein in Germany (see page 50).

RIGHT
For the decoration of the Gallery, Walpole enlisted suggestions from his "committee of taste" ▶

FOLLOWING DOUBLE SPREAD
The neo-Gothic castle built by Walpole was about ten times larger than the original 17th century villa ▶▶

The replication of particular stylistic forms shows that the architect was not guided by building techniques or the need to satisfy specific requirements, but only the wish to create a certain atmosphere. When designing their castles, owners were only interested in the visual forms of the late Gothic without worrying about the concepts that dictated these forms. The library fireplace, for example, is clearly inspired by Gothic sepulchral monuments. The guiding motto was that "what pleases is always beautiful". The original building techniques of Gothic architecture were quite outdated by now, the carved masonry becoming mere stucco decoration without any structural function.

It is clear that Walpole reflected the spirit of the time when he rebuilt Strawberry Hill. The castle was already a famous sight during his own lifetime, and was even better known than his literary work. Walpole was not the only person behind the success of the Gothic Revival, but his imaginative fantasy at Strawberry Hill undoubtedly played an important part.

In 2010, Strawberry Hill was re-opened to the public after a comprehensive restoration.

◀ **LEFT**
The library at Strawberry Hill. The whole building played an important part in the 18th century Gothic Revival

Horace Walpole the writer

Walpole was a politician by profession, but he only occupied minor posts in the government, usually obtained through the influence of his father, Prime Minister Robert Walpole. Horace Walpole's field of interest was cultural rather than political. His interest in architecture is remembered in Strawberry Hill. He was also an enthusiastic collector of art and curiosities, but above all he was a writer.

The Castle of Otranto, published by Walpole in 1765, marked the beginning of his literary reputation. The novel is set in 13th century Italy, but the thematic symbol, namely a castle and its architecture, are very reminiscent of Strawberry Hill. Mysterious things happen, terrible powers are at work, pictures become alive, doors creak and thunder is all around. Horace Walpole's novel was one of the first Gothic novels, a variation on the English novel towards the end of the 18th century. It was Walpole himself who first used the term "Gothic novel" to describe the book, because his enthusiasm for the Middle Ages and for anything Gothic is as evident in his novel as it is in his house.

Tower of London and Dover Castle

According to legend, the monarchy will only survive while the ravens remain in the Tower of London. In reality, the birds can hardly fly away since their wings are clipped, and this is why they must be fed every day by their keepers. The money for their food is included in the defense budget and every raven that dies becomes an honorary member of the army, because it will have contributed to the continued survival of the monarchy by its presence in the Tower.

The Tower itself has contributed to the survival of the monarchy throughout the centuries, not only as a fortress but as a royal residence, a place of execution, a prison and as a secure place to keep the crown jewels. The best-preserved and most important Norman fortress in England has been attacked and besieged in the past, but never captured.

In the center of a complex of 17 acres stands the White Tower, built from light-colored stone imported from Caen in Normandy by William the Conqueror. He built it in 1078, modelling it on the bastions of northern France. It was a residence providing protection against the Anglo-Saxons who threatened to rebel against their new ruler.

The tower is 100 ft high and built in accordance with the classical model of the donjon or keep. The storerooms and stables are on the ground floor, with the living quarters for soldiers and servants on the first floor. A raised entrance leads to the second floor that contains the official state rooms. The third or top floor houses the royal apartments and assembly rooms. The chapel on the second floor has a simple, barrel-vaulted ceiling and massive columns supporting a gallery. It is the oldest church in London.

Some 150 years later, Henry III built the inner circle of walls as additional protection while his son Edward I further strengthened the fortress by building a moat, an outer ring of walls with towers overlooking the Thames as well as two bastions. The Waterloo Barracks accommodates the Yeomen Warders, known as Beefeaters, and the crown jewels. They were built in 1845 under the authority of the general and politician the Duke of Wellington.

RIGHT
Royal residence, place of execution, prison and secure home of the crown jewels – the Tower of London has had many uses ▶

◀ LEFT
One of many rooms exhibited inside the Tower of London with period design and furnishing

ENTRY TO THE TRAITORS' GATE

A Norman fortress in Dover

Traditionally, Dover has always been the "gateway" between the continent and the capital, London. William the Conqueror followed the same route with the Norman invasion of 1066. In the same way that William had protected himself and his new territory in London by building the Tower of London, Henry II later built the Norman fortress in Dover to protect the strategically most important stretch of coast in England.

Dover Castle rises threateningly on the cliffs high above the town. Erected in 1168, it was constantly enlarged and during the Middle Ages it had become one of the most modern fortresses in Europe. The Norman keep is built in the center of the fortress, protected by several rows of fortifications with square watchtowers. Earthworks were erected between the rows of walls as additional obstacles.

◀ **LEFT**
Dover Castle, bulwark
against a possible
invasion

Windsor Castle

One of the most famous castles in the world, built on a rocky outcrop, Windsor Castle dominates the town of Windsor. It has a history of almost one thousand years and has witnessed all the ups and downs of the English monarchy. Since it was built by William the Conqueror, it has been the family seat of the English royal family.

After conquering England in the 11th century, William the Conqueror set about securing his new territory and his power. In about 1078, at the same time as he built the Tower of London (see page 262), he also built Windsor Castle as a fortress in Windsor, one of a series of defensive castles constructed around the capital.

Throughout the centuries, the English monarchs have gradually enlarged the castle to meet new standards of comfort and security. They have also added state rooms and apartments befitting the residence of a royal family, turning the fortress into a magnificent palace.

The most radical changes were made in the 12th and 13th century when the wooden buildings and palisades were replaced by stone buildings and walls, and the keep was replaced by the Round Tower. Since then the Round Tower has marked the division between the Upper and the Lower Wards. St George's Chapel was built in the Lower Ward between 1475 and 1525, while in 1683, Charles II rebuilt the castle in Baroque style. At the beginning of the 19th century, George IV commissioned the architect Jeffrey Wyatville to redesign the castle. These were to be the last major changes, giving Windsor Castle its present-day appearance.

From the outside, the castle looks like a formidable, romantic fortress, while it surprises visitors with its sumptuous, magnificent interior decoration. When the queen is in residence, the Royal Standard is hoisted on the Round Tower. This tends to be mainly in early summer, Christmas and Easter. So long as the Queen is not in residence, the State Apartments are open to the public. They include the Grand Staircase, the Large Hall, the Ballroom,

RIGHT
Remains of the past, the watchtowers of Windsor castle ▶

◀ The Changing of the Guard still takes place in honor of the queen on the castle's parade ground

the Waterloo Chamber, the Queen's Drawing Room and the Royal Bedrooms. Many of the rooms are still decorated with Baroque wall paintings by Antonio Verrio. All the apartments contain precious works of art because Queen Elizabeth owns one of the largest private collections of art. However, there are also magnificent works of art in other parts of the castle, such as in the George IV Tower, so it is well worth visiting the castle even when the State Apartments are not open to the public.

Simple magnificence

One of the most important places of interest in Windsor Castle is St George's Chapel, a masterpiece of perpendicular Gothic. This is a wonderful example of English late-Gothic, characterised by its emphasis on vertical elements. The south-facing facade with its turrets and pillars is particularly handsome. The interior of the chapel is impressive yet restrained at the same time. It has a wonderful fan vaulted ceiling and a magnificent west window of stained glass, composed of 75 separate lights. These represent kings, bishops, popes and saints, forming a real synthesis of the arts. It is the chapel of the Order of the Garter, the order of chivalry founded by Edward III in 1348.

◀ **LEFT**
The castle has been altered and extended many times during its 1,000 year history

Cawdor Castle

Cawdor Castle, the scene of the crime: Macbeth murders King Duncan in order to become king himself. This is a short summary of Shakespeare's famous tragedy in five acts, a play that makes Cawdor Castle a magnet for literary-minded visitors. Sadly, the legend is not true.

"Duncan did not die in our castle, and nor was he treacherously murdered in bed. Macbeth slew him in the Battle of Elgin in 1040. In fact, the oldest part of castle, the central tower, dates only from the 14th century, and the rest from the 17th century." With this remark, visitors to Cawdor Castle are corrected in their romantic misinterpretation by members of the family, who also give them a quick lesson in Scottish history. Shakespeare borrowed the Macbeth story from the famous Chronicles of England, Scotland and Ireland (1587) by Ralph Holinshed and reworked it between 1606 till 1611 so as to improve its "dramatic" effect, thereby ignoring the real facts.

And yet, Cawdor Castle looks as if it could be the scene of the king's murder! The castle is surrounded by a park and woodland, secured by a small river on one side and a moat with drawbridge on the other. Earthworks surround the bailey, and the tower with its mighty walls looks fortified. The facades with their battlements are imposing, while the turrets with cone-shaped roofs and the graduated gables add a romantic touch. All this would be a perfect setting for Macbeth.

In fact, it is these particular features, characteristic of the Scottish baronial style, that indicate that the castle was built several centuries after Macbeth's time. When he lived, castles in Scotland were still tower houses. These mostly square, peel towers were often surrounded by a wall and built for defensive purposes. The concept of domestic comfort did not exist in the Scottish castles at the time; it only became a reality with the introduction of the Scottish baronial style. Thus, behind the massive walls of Cawdor are magnificently furnished rooms. However, the family has not banished Shakespeare entirely – there is a drawing of Macbeth by Salvador Dali.

Otherwise, the castle houses traditional family memorabilia such as the obligatory gallery of ancestors and ancient weapons, as well as a very contemporary Aikido belt that belonged to the 24th Thane of Cawdor who died in 1993. The castle is surrounded by flower gardens that include a collection of some thirty species of thistles as well as a typical Scottish maze, made from holly.

RIGHT
Cawdor Castle is surrounded by unpretentious gardens which harmonize perfectly with the harsh Scottish landscape ▶

◀ **LEFT**
One of the thirthy species of thistles in Cawdor Castle's gardens

CULZEAN CASTLE

Martial on the outside, delicate on the inside – Culzean Castle combines the apparently irreconcilable in such a remarkable way that the Royal Bank of Scotland chose it to decorate its five-pound notes.

Situated south of Ayr in the Lowlands of Scotland, Culzean Castle was designed by the Scottish architect Robert Adam and built between 1777 and 1792. Even the setting of the former estate of the Earl of Cassillis, with Scotland's wild and rocky coast on the one side, and a carefully tended garden hinting at the Mediterranean with palms and flowers on the other, is a clue that opposites are combined throughout this castle.

The exterior face presented to visitors is the essence of strict fortified architecture with defensive corner and side towers, battlements and embrasure windows in the plain style of medieval fortresses. The windows are generally on the small side, and the roof finishes in a parapet. Thus the surprise on stepping inside is even greater, and a visit is certainly among the highlights of a trip to Scotland. The interior is of classical elegance, with Italian nuances forming a fascinating contrast to the unpretentious exterior. Robert Adam was the architect as well as the interior designer, and he wanted his building to radiate grace and beauty.

On entering, the gaze is inevitably drawn to the Oval Staircase, bedecked in red carpet. Its pillared gallery extending over two floors makes it a masterpiece of classical interior architecture. The staircase gives access to the rest of the tastefully decorated rooms, which all follow an overall aesthetic concept down to the last detail.

The most splendid room must be the Circular Saloon, which manages to combine almost every variety of the Adam style. Graceful leaf and tendril ornaments, evidence of Adam's Italian training, run throughout the room, framing the fireplace and door. Pastel shades of blue, green, and pink underline the delicacy of the decorative elements. The gaze is drawn upwards by the fine stucco ceiling, because its basic geometric patterns are developed into ornamental fields that are reflected in the rest of the room and in the round carpet. Little niches loosen up the room's hermetic structure. The interior fittings in the

RIGHT
The outside of the castle, which gives no hint of the classical elegance within ▶

FOLLOWING DOUBLE SPREAD
Mediterranean flair in the Scottish Lowlands, with palms and flowers forming a contrast to the austere castle ▶▶

◀ **LEFT**
Symbols of defensive readiness: cannons in front of Culzean Castle

room also include garlanded mirrors, wall lights and standard lamps in the form of rams with hooves and heads designed by Robert Adam, who did not want to leave anything to chance in the effect created by the room.

For some visitors in the 21st century, brought up on the clear, straight line designs of the present, this play of colors and forms may appear a little exaggerated at first, perhaps even too sugary-sweet. Nevertheless, they must also acknowledge the harmony with which one thing runs into the next, and the unshakeable confidence with which Adam indulged his fantasy in patterns, decorations and colors. The castle is still inhabited since it serves Scotland as "National Guest House". When members of the Kennedy clan, remotedly related to John F. Kennedy, gave Culzean to the National Trust for Scotland in 1945, it gave a lifelong interest in the apartment on the top floor to General Dwight D. Eisenhower, as a thank-you from the people of Scotland. Eisenhower visited the apartment several times during his life. In 2011, the castle was re-opened to the public after extensive renovations.

A revolutionary designer of his time: Robert Adam

Robert Adam was born in Kirkcaldy in Scotland on 3 July 1728. His father William was then Scotland's leading architect and, as was usual at that time, introduced his son to the profession. Although Robert had already learnt something of the classical style from his father, his passion for classicism began in 1754 when he went to study in Italy. Over the next four years he came to know Hellenic-Roman architecture and art, reveling in its forms and ornaments. He was able not just to copy them but to give them a style of their own, one that could not belie his Scottish origins.

On his return, Adam moved to London, thinking that Scotland would be too parochial for his career plans. This was a clever choice, because there he was quickly able to surpass his father's success. Robert Adam became architect to King George III in 1761. As a perfectionist, Adam always regarded and designed a building as a whole, including the interior room fittings and, as in Culzean, he became involved in the smallest details, down to the door knobs. In order to ensure that these fine details really did look as he imagined them, he established the firm William Adam & Company in 1764 to produce them. This family enterprise, which employed all of Robert's siblings, rapidly grew into a large company with a workforce of some 2,000 people. His interior room designs in particular made Robert Adam and his Adam style internationally famous, as far afield as the United States and Russia.

Holyrood Palace

In the early 12th century when Edinburgh was the capital of the Scottish monarchs, David I, the son of Queen Margaret the Saint, went hunting on a Sunday, which was forbidden. He was almost gored to death by the deer's antlers, but he was miraculously saved by the Holy Cross, the Holyrood. In grateful acknowledgement, he founded Holyrood Abbey on the spot in 1218 and later built the original Holyrood Palace next to it.

The origins of Holyrood are modest. It used to be a former guesthouse of the neighboring Holyrood Abbey, where the first kings of Scotland sometimes spent the night. Between 1528 and 1532 James V, Mary Stuart's father, built Holyrood's northwest tower as a tower house with battlements and round towers at each of the four corners. Adjoining it was the longer west wing with two interior courtyards.

Between 1671 and 1679, Charles II asked the architect William Bruce to renovate and restore the castle, which had suffered serious damage under Cromwell and had been partially destroyed by two fires. Even though finances were tight, Bruce had to solve the problem of how to restore the old walls in contemporary style while meeting the requirements of comfort. The result was a palace that successfully combined historical and contemporary architectural styles. The architect merged two distinct architectural styles, the Italian Palladian style to which he had been introduced by his colleague Inigo Jones, and the elegance of the early French Baroque castles that he had visited himself.

William Bruce used the plan of James I's tower house and west wing and built a counterpart to the northwest wing of the old castle. He linked the two towers, using a lower building with a roof balustrade. He located the main entrance in the middle of this lower building, emphasized by two Doric columns and a raised entablature bearing the date of completion, 1680. The facade overlooking the interior courtyard is built in classical-Palladian style and divided into three sections with Doric, Ionic and Corinthian pilasters. The facade is the architectural expression of the Auld Alliance between Scotland and France. In other words, although not homogeneous, it skillfully combines the massiveness of the Scottish tower house with French elegance.

The interior is decorated in Anglo-Flemish style, the latest fashion at the time. The ceiling paintings and coat-of-arms are by the Dutch painter Jacob de Wet, while the carvings decorating the fireplace and doors are by his fellow countryman Jan Vansantvoort. The Gobelin tapestries came Brussels, Flanders and Paris.

The renovation of the forecourt, which started in 2016, will be completed in 2018.

RIGHT
The Palace of Holyrood is a successful combination of the Italian Palladian style and the elegance of French baroque ▶

STIRLING CASTLE

Scotland's history rests on two rocks, Edinburgh and Stirling. This familiar observation reflects the importance of the Scottish royal house of the Stuarts, and their seat, Stirling Castle.

The city of Stirling is situated west of Edinburgh on the border between the Lowlands and the Highlands, on the Firth of Forth. The castle is built on a rocky outcrop and dominates the town below. The location was strategically so secure that all the royal children of the House of Stuart were brought up here, since Stirling Castle was deemed to be much safer than Edinburgh.

The center of the fortress is the palace near the upper bailey, which James V built round a courtyard between 1538 and 1542. The audience hall is decorated with very ornate wooden medallions, the Stirling Heads, representing the kings of Scotland. The interior courtyard is embellished with sculptures placed in niches between the windows. Demons and devils carry mythological figures on columns while the stone statues of animals decorating the parapet wall act as gargoyles. All this makes the palace in Stirling Castle a magnificent example of Scottish early Renaissance with strong French influences. The Great Hall was built at the end of the 15th century under James III. This fine Gothic hall with music gallery and hammer-beam roof was conceived as a multi-purpose room, for ceremonies and sessions of Parliament but certainly not for use as barracks – although that is what it was used for at the end of the 18th century.

Adjoining the Great Hall is the chapel. It was renovated by James VI in 1594 for his son's christening.

The key to Scotland

Stirling Castle was known as the key to Scotland because of its strategic location on a rocky outcrop. From here, the Stuarts were able to control the fertile plain around the Firth of Forth and see enemies approaching from a great distance, enabling them to prepare a suitable reception for those bold enough to attack. Numerous battles were fought near Stirling Castle. In 1297, William Wallace triumphed over the English, and Robert the Bruce won the decisive battle of the Wars of Independence against Edward II at Bannockburn in 1314 when 8,000 Scots fought 20,000 English. The Scots captured the entire army as well as much money and many weapons.

RIGHT
Stirling Castle is strategically situated on the border between the Highlands and the Lowlands, enabling the Stuarts to see enemies approaching from afar ▶

GRIPSHOLM CASTLE, LAKE MÄLAREN

"It was a brilliantly clear day. The castle, built from red brick, stood there in all its glory, its round cupolas rising against the blue sky. It was a massive, noble, well-designed fortress." This description comes from the German novel Schloss Gripsholm by Kurt Tucholsky, published in 1931, which made this beautiful Vasa castle better known outside Sweden.

At the end of the 14th century Bo Jonsson Grip, the lord high steward, built a castle on a small island in Lake Mälaren, about 31 miles west of the Swedish capital, Stockholm. He named it Gripsholm after his heraldic beast, the griffin (grip in Swedish) and the island (holme) on which it was built. Stockholm had an important strategic location, but the castle was destroyed in a fire 50 years later.

After having been the property of the monastery of Mariefred, the ruins of the castle were seized by Gustav Erikson Vasa. In 1523, he was elected King Gustav I of Sweden, but his position in Sweden, which he had declared independent of Denmark, was still insecure. He therefore found it advisable to build fortified castles in the region. The site of the Gripsholm ruins suited Vasa as they had Bo Jonnson Grip before him. In 1537, he commissioned the German architect Henrik von Cöllen to build him a royal castle. Von Cöllen was an experienced architect who had already built several castles.

Decades went by before Gripsholm was finally completed. The result was an irregularly shaped castle with four mighty round peel towers with walls 10 to 13 feet thick. Gustav Vasa moved into the castle while it was still being built and lived there for a few years, but he died long before it was completed. Nor was it finished by his successors, Erik XIV and Johann III. Eventually, modern military warfare overwhelmed the old defensive provisions of the castle. However, its defense capabilities were never tested, and during the following centuries it was used as a residence and gradually rebuilt as a palace.

The first monarch to alter the old fortress was Karl IX who rebuilt the first floor in Renaissance style. In addition, the Vasa Tower was converted into a small residential wing. This Karl IX Wing stands in the forework whose main gate was built in 1596.

The Queen's Wing was erected in 1690 next to the Theatre Tower. In the 17th century, it was used almost exclusively by Swedish queens as a widow's retreat. It was Queen Lovisa Ulrika who added the final touches to the fortress of Gripsholm in 1744 that turned it into Gripsholm Castle. She added the elegant cupolas to complete the towers, giving the castle the

RIGHT
On sunny days, the brilliant red bricks of the castle stand out beautifully against the blues of the sky and Lake Mälaren ▶

FOLLOWING DOUBLE SPREAD
The most beautiful view of Gripsholm Castle is from the shore at Mariefred, the little town nearby ▶▶

distinctive, imposing appearance it has today. Thirty years later Gripsholm achieved royal status again when Gustav III chose it as his residence. He added a story to the Queen's Wing and decorated some of the rooms in the early classical Gustavian style. In addition, he built a theatre in the church tower whose auditorium was in the tower while the stage and side rooms were in the Queen's Wing. The original furnishings were replaced in 1781–83 – with more modern ones by Erik Palmstedt after only ten years. The theatre is a masterpiece of early classical interior decoration and is well preserved because it is hardly ever used. Tucholsky was filled with admiration, as is apparent in his novel: "But the most beautiful part was the theatre. There was a small theatre in the castle, probably so that they would not get bored during sieges."

The German writer also noticed something else when he first went to Gripsholm: "There were many beautiful paintings in the castle. But they did not mean anything to me." This was hardly surprising – he would have had to be an expert in Swedish history to recognize the faces in the paintings. In the first half of the 19th century King Karl XIV Johann collected portraits of famous Swedish men and women to create a "Pantheon of Swedish History." The monarch thus laid the foundation of the largest portrait gallery in Sweden – one of the most important in Europe.

The collection includes over 3,500 portraits and is still being supplemented. New paintings of outstanding personalities are added to the collection on the recommendation of the government. Naturally, not all the paintings can be on show in the castle, which is managed by the National Museum and Royal Art Collection.

The paintings of middle-class citizens after 1809 are usually stored in the buildings to the west of the castle island.

◄ LEFT
Window through the thick walls at Gripsholm castle

Kurt Tucholsky in Sweden

The German author and journalist, born in 1890, was a theatre and literary critic who also wrote essays, poetry and cabaret scripts of great accuracy and biting irony. He supported left-wing humanism and opposed corruption, nationalism and militarism. In 1929, he moved to Sweden and spent a long time at Gripsholm Castle. In 1933, he was deprived of his German citizenship by the National Socialists. He is buried in the cemetery in Mariefred, the small town near Gripsholm Castle that his work had also made famous.

ROYAL PALACE, STOCKHOLM

The Royal Palace is built on the island of Stadsholmen in the center of Stockholm, the Swedish capital built on islands and peninsulas in Lake Mälaren on the Baltic Sea. The Baroque castle, situated in the old town, seems rather out of place here. It is the largest castle in the world still used as a residence by a head of state.

The original building on the site of the present Royal Palace was the Tre Kronor fortress erected in the late 13th century. At the end of the 17th century, it was decided that the old fortress needed modernizing, and so Nicodemus Tessin the Younger built a new Baroque wing to the north between 1690 and 1695. The medieval complex was entirely destroyed by fire two years later, in 1697, and the new Baroque wing was the only part to survive. This sealed the fate of Tre Kronor. In the same year, what remained of the fortress was pulled

down to the foundations, which can still be seen in the cellars of the present palace. The new palace was to consist of four wings, including the "old" north wing which was incorporated in the new design. Construction of the new castle was often interrupted because Kharles XII gave financial precedence to the needs of the war he was waging against Poland, Russia and Denmark. After Tessin's death in 1728, Carl HŹrleman took over the project and completed it in 1770.

The result was an imposing castle with four wings, built in an eclectic Baroque style already somewhat outdated by then. The facades are not as lavishly decorated or detailed as other Baroque palaces but rather plain and strict. As a result, they are majestic and a little cold, an impression is further emphasized by the interior facades of the four three-storied main buildings that form an almost square courtyard. Each building is covered by a nearly flat roof, and decorated by a plain stone balustrade. There are no ornamental sculptures, cupolas or triangular pediments, just simple elegance.

Adjoining the east or garden front are two charming smaller wings of only one floor, flanking a half-open garden whose rectangular terrace is linked to the wa-

RIGHT
The Throne Room in baroque style ▶

◀ **LEFT**
Well-guarded, as befits a Royal Palace still used for official functions

ter's edge by steps. It is counterbalanced by the forecourt on the west front. The main courtyard is bordered by arcades. These are unfortunately screened by a wall from a busy road so that the impression of openness no longer exists. Nevertheless, these arcades still provide a suitable setting for official receptions and the regular parades of the guard.

In contrast to the exterior, the interior decoration and furnishings reflected the fashion of the time and the new stylistic developments of Rococo and early Classicism.

In the 19th and 20th centuries, some rooms were refurnished in contemporary style but on the whole, the furniture and decoration have remained as they were in the 18th century.

In the south wing is the King's Throne Room, built in late Baroque style after Tessin's plans but with the addition of a few Rococo pieces by Horleman. On the other hand, the silver throne that immediately attracts the eye was crafted in Augsburg in 1640, while the two marble statues on each side of it are more recent, dating from 1844 and carved by Niklas Byström.

The castle chapel, also in the south wing, dates from the same period as the Throne Room. The altar with its large stone relief was designed by Tessin but not completed by him. It was finished by Tobias Sergel in 1799. The paintings on the ceiling and the stuccowork were designed by French artists.

The castle is no longer the permanent residence of the Swedish kings but is now a museum housing the treasure chamber, the royal armory and other royal collections. The treasure chamber is in the south wing and in it the state regalia of the Swedish kings are displayed. Also in the south wing, in the cellar vault, is the royal armory. This contains many royal and military exhibits: armor, weapons, ornate parade coaches, clothes for the coronation and even the costume that Gustav III was wearing when he was murdered during a fancy-dress ball in 1792. The collections dating from the 17th century are unique in Europe.

In 1781, when the whole world was fascinated by classical antiquity, the Italian artist Francesco Piranesi purchased numerous antique sculptures on behalf of Gustavus III. These sculptures form the basis of the "Antique Museum Gustav III," which opened at the end of the 18th century and is now housed in the north wing.

The Royal Palace has over 600 rooms, many of which are open to the public, although King Karl XVI Gustav carries out his official duties in this building. (The Swedish king now has representative and ceremonial functions but no political power.) Many of the state rooms are open to the public unless they are being used for official receptions and banquets or similar events. Naturally, the king's private apartments and study are always closed to the public.

◀◀ **PREVIOUS DOUBLE SPREAD**
The Royal Palace is built on the island of Stadsholmen in Lake Mälaren

◀ **LEFT**
A military parade in front of the palace in honor of the royal family

AMALIENBORG PALACE

Amalienborg Slot, as it is called in Danish, has been the residence of the Danish kings since 1794. It consists of four separate palaces, arranged around the octagonal Amalienborg Slotplads with an equestrian statue of Frederick V in the middle. Recognized as the high point of Danish Rococo, it is an unusual residence both in its conception and in the history of its origins.

When the 300th jubilee of the House of Oldenburg was just round the corner in 1749, Frederick V of Denmark had an extravagant idea to celebrate the occasion: he would build a new district of the Danish capital in Copenhagen, which would be named Frederikstaden after him. The Amalienborg area – where the now ruined Italianate pleasure palace of Sophie Amalienborg stood – was chosen as the site for the new district, which was to have two main axes. A square with a monument would be built at the intersection of these two axes, the Amalienborg Slotplads or Palace Square. Because of the serious fire that had damaged the town in 1728, special precautions were taken to ensure the safety of the new town – such as the removal of timber yards and a ban on bakeries, breweries and distilleries.

The planning of the new district was entrusted to the court architect Nicolai Eigtved, a pupil of Matthäus Daniel Pöpplemann who also designed the Amalienborg Palace and square. The result was four identical main buildings that formed an octagonal open space together with their corner pavilions. Each palace has two-and-a-half floors, with a mezzanine floor under the roof. The facade is embellished with an eye-catching, central projecting part, whose three tall, arched windows take up the space across the top, main and mezzanine floors and open up onto the first floor behind. Six Ionic columns frame the windows and support the projecting part of the roof balustrade, decorated with large coat-of-arms that from afar looks a little like a small pediment. The rest of the roof balustrade was decorated with vases, figures and busts by court artist Johann Christoph Petzold. Together with Jacob Fortling, he was responsible for decorating the facades, including the cornices, windows and door frames, in a fairly sober, understated manner. Accordingly, the side projecting parts do not emerge very far beyond the main facade, and they only differ through having slightly more elaborate decoration.

Another unusual aspect of the history of the castle is the fact that the four palaces did not at first belong to the royal family. It is true that Frederick had had the idea, chosen the land and advised on the planning, but he did not want to build it himself. Instead, in 1750, he offered the land to four prominent, prosperous men of Copenhagen: Privy Councillor Joachim von Brockdorff, Count C. F. von Levetzau, Baron Severin Leopoldus Lovenskjold and Lord Marshall Count Adam Gotlob Moltke. This gift came with a tax remission for the next forty years,

RIGHT
Amalienborg Palace
Interior ▶

FOLLOWING DOUBLE SPREAD
After a fire destroyed the royal palace of Christianborg in 1794, a group of four noble palaces became the official residence of the Danish royal family ▶▶

because the four men, as future owners of the buildings, were also expected to incur some extra expenses that otherwise would have been borne by the king. Then from 1794 onwards, the royal family began to buy up the palaces one by one in order to use them as an official royal residence.

Because of the separate ownership of the palaces, they are considerably different inside although similar externally. The most sumptuous palace is that to the southwest, which belonged to Moltke. It is known what the original interior looked like from documents relating to the fire insurance dating from 1754. In the hall "there are eight free-standing columns of the Corinthian order with pilaster strips on the walls behind, all of marble and very beautifully arranged. The walls and ceiling are decorated with decorative stucco, the door frames are also in marble..." However, the capitals were carved out of wood because that was cheaper and quicker to make.

The dining-room was decorated in 1757 by Nicolas-Henri Jardin, the director of the Copenhagen Academy of Arts. The walls are of white and gold with Ionic pilasters and free-standing columns, gilt trophies and vases that were then the latest fashion. Today the ensemble is recognized as one of the highlights of classical interior decoration in Europe.

In Danish Rococo, walls were traditionally decorated with Gobelin tapestries and painted wallpaper but Count Moltke had other ideas for his banqueting hall, which he decorated with wood panelling: "The walls are covered with precious panelling and beautiful, ornate carvings that are gilded like all the panel moldings. The panelling is painted in white lacquer. They are embellished with beautifully carved portraits of Your Royal Majesties in gilt frames ...and five works representing science, geometry, sculpture, painting and mathematics. ... The ceiling is decorated with stucco with a rosette in the center, all of which is gilded. The floor is pinc and oak parquet..." This magnificent room is further embellished with paintings above the doors that Moltke himself commissioned from the Paris studio of his friend François Boucher. Five carry the painter's signature.

The little mermaid

The symbol of Copenhagen is not a magnificent building as it is in many other cities, but a graceful statue called "The little mermaid" after Hans Christian Anderson's fairy-tale of the same name. This bronze figure was made in 1908 by Edvard Eriksen. It is situated near the harbor, north of the Amalienborg castle.

Marienburg

Hradc˘any, the Kremlin, Marienburg: the largest castle complexes in Europe. Marienburg may only be third in order of importance, but it is also the largest brick building in Europe. For the Poles it is one of the most important historical buildings in the country and is virtually considered the holy shrine ot the Polish people.

The city of Malbork (originally the German Marienburg) is situated on the Nogat River, about 37 miles southeast of Danzig. Some 825 years ago the Teutonic Order selected this site to ensure its control over the Vistula by building a fortress and town there. The construction of the fortress on the bank of the Nogat River began in 1274. It took about thirty years to complete the multi-storied, almost square building.

The fortress consists of four wings with a battlemented parapet under the crest of the roof, small corner turrets and a square keep. It was used as a monastery by the knights of the Order as early as 1280, because they moved the location while the fortress was still in the process of being built. The ground floor contained the domestic offices while the first floor of the north wing had the chapter room, and the Mariankirche that occupied two floors. The bedrooms of the knights were in the east wing, while the treasure chambers and apartments were in the west wing. The second floor was devoted to storerooms, the refectory, the assembly hall and knights' dining room. In 1309, the Grand Masters of the Teutonic Order moved its residence from Venice to Marienburg. They enlarged the fortress and added a cloister built in the inner courtyard as a gallery across two floors and round the four wings. The chapel in the north wing was extended in an easterly direction between 1331 and 1344 and became the castle church of St Mary.

While the fortress was being enlarged, the central castle was built in 1330 to provide a suitably luxurious, comfortable residence for the Grand Master. Separated from the fortress by its own moat and a drawbridge, tower gate and keep with portcullis, it was better protected than the rest of the castle. Its Large Refectory was one of the largest banqueting halls in Europe at the time – a hall 98 ft long and 49 ft wide with a star-ribbed vault supported by three columns.

At the end of the 14th century, a very fine palace was built for the Grand Master, albeit a little smaller than the other two castles. Bay windows embellish its facade while the apartments of the Grand Master are decorated with floral ornaments. It also has a large summer refectory with a remarkable ribbed vault, spectacularly supported by a single central column, and a winter refectory that is smaller so that it could be heated more easily. The imposing Marienburg complex is completed by St Lorenzkirche and buildings for the domestic offices, as well as various bulwarks and entrenchments, situated to the north of the central castle.

RIGHT
Bridge leading to the castle ▶

FOLLOWING DOUBLE SPREAD
View from the west across the Nogat of the incomparable brick buildings of the castle at Marienburg ▶▶

NEXT DOUBLE SPREAD
The ribbed vault of the summer refectory, supported by a single column ▶▶

PAVLOVSK

Like all self-respecting European rulers, the Russian tsars also built summer residences expressing not only splendor and power but also the artistic sense of the inhabitants. About 19 miles southwest of St Petersburg is the palace of Pavlovsk, surrounded by an English-style landscaped garden.

In 1777, Catherine II presented the vast forested areas to the southwest of St Petersburg to her son Paul I and his wife Maria Feodorovna as a gift on the birth of their son, the future Tsar Alexander I. Pavlovsk, named after Paul I, was built five years later according to the plans of the Scottish architect Charles Cameron. It was a classic summer residence, strongly inspired by English country houses and the villas designed by the Italian architect Andrea Palladio (1508–80), who was famous for his two-storied facades with columns inspired by ancient Rome.

The cube-shaped central block of the palace is approached from the oval courtyard, with its central statue of Paul I. A portico adorned with Corinthian columns leads the eye upward towards a rotunda consisting of 64 columns, covered with a flattened cupola that dominates the three-storied building. The garden front overlooking the park has a portico with a pediment. Cameron skillfully used the incidence of light entering through the cupola to illuminate the circular Italian Hall below it, making it the center of the palace. Everything in this room is reminiscent of ancient Rome, while in the Grecian Hall copies of ancient statues and imitation green marble columns bring ancient Greece back to life. A magnificent staircase leads to the state hall of the upper story, decorated by Vincenzo Brenna with symbols of battle and war.

Brenna also decorated the imposing rooms next to the Greek room, namely the Hall of Peace and the Hall of War. The former is decorated with cornucopias, flower garlands and musical instruments. It leads to a several exquisitely decorated apartments belonging to Maria Feodorovna that are arranged in enfilade, so that when the doors are open it is possible to see through them all to the last room. The Hall of War is decorated accordingly and leads to a similar enfilade of Paul I's apartments.

The central building is flanked on each side by a twostoried gallery with columns, arranged to form an elegant curve. They link the central part of the building with the outer wing pavilions whose extensions mark the boundary of the courtyard. The galleries and wings originally had one story less than they do now; they were enlarged by Vincenzo Brenna in 1797.

RIGHT
The summer residence of the tsar lies in a garden landscaped in the English style ▶

◀ **LEFT**
Stone lion at the entrance to the palace

The galleries contain a library and a collection of paintings. The picture gallery leads to the throne room whose ceiling was decorated by the Russian set designer Pietro Gonzaga. The painting shows an open heaven above a classical building. Pietro Gonzaga was also responsible for the architectural landscapes with perspectives in the curved galleries overlooking the park.

The park was designed as a landscape garden in the English style popular at the time. Inspired by the Romantic Movement, this garden style was developed in England in the 18th century, and is therefore often described simply as an 'English garden.' The aim was to create a landscape that appeared as natural as possible, taking the natural topographical conditions into consideration but ensuring the harmonious alternation of large meadows, single trees, groups of trees and shrubs, man-made springs, paths, monuments and picturesque buildings. Goethe described this as a "succession of aesthetic images." Artificial ruins, temples and pavilions were the classic ways of "furnishing" a landscaped garden.

Maria Feodorovna was personally interested in the design of the park surrounding Pavlovsk and she created romantic theme-landscapes. The design of the garden certainly did not suffer from the fact that experienced architects such as Cameron, Brenna and Andrej Woronichin took no part in it. The oldest building in the park is also the most important. It is the Temple of Friendship (1780–82), designed by Charles Cameron. This small rotunda not far from the palace stands on a loop of the Slawjanka River. Its enclosed inner room contains a sculpture of Catherine II posed as the goddess Ceres, surrounded by a row of Doric columns and a frieze on the wall, depicting garlands and dolphins symbolizing friendship.

Cameron also designed the Temple of Apollo (a colonnade that was left as a romantic ruin after its collapse in 1817), the Cold Bath and the Voliere, a building with a domed room in the center. He also built the Pavilion of the Three Graces, which was the last building designed by the Scottish architect in St Petersburg and its surroundings.

Pavlovsk's most recent past

During World War II, Pavlovsk was devastated by the German armed forces, like most of the residences of the tsars. As the soldiers withdrew in 1944, they cleared the park and the palace was burned out. Luckily the art treasures had been brought to Leningrad (as St Petersburg was then called) where they were kept in safety for posterity. The restoration was costly and was not finished until the last decade of the 20th century.

Winter Palace, St Petersburg

A total of 1,050 rooms with a floor area of 11 acres, 1,945 windows, 1,886 doors and 117 stairs: these figures alone illustrate the size of this palace. The Baroque residence of the Russian tsars is a gigantic monument to their power and perfectly suited to house the vast, incomparable collections of the Hermitage.

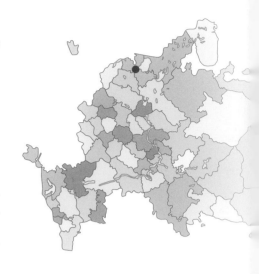

The north facade of the Winter Palace is reflected in the water of the Neva River, on the "large side" of the city. The view of the palace with its columns arranged in two superimposed rows, breaking up the facade while also unifying it with their regular sequence, is really wonderful. The architect Bartolomeo Rastrelli also took the effect of a distant view into account when designing the south facade, seen from the main Covrtyard. Here visitors have the opportunity of seeing the rich decoration of the facade close at hand. Although the facades of the four wings arranged around the rectangular main courtyard are all different from each other, the Winter Palace has a homogeneous appearance. This is because Rastrelli also added elements in common, such as the columns in two superimposed rows that break up the facades, and the unifying roof balustrade adorned with numerous statues.

Although the first stone of the Winter Palace was laid in 1711, building only began in 1754 when Elizabeth I, the daughter of Peter the Great, approved – Rastrelli's plans were the only ones she liked. Rastrelli (c. 1700–71) left his mark on St Petersburg with his elegant buildings but he was unable to complete his last and most important commission, so the ornamentation of the building was designed by a number of other architects, commissioned by Catherine II (1729–96). Vallin de la Mothes, Antonio Rinaldi, Jurij Felten, Giacomo Quarenghi, Carlo Rossi, Wassilij Stassow, Auguste Montferrand: all these St Petersburg architects contributed to the interior decoration of the Winter Palace.

On the first floor, there are still a few rooms with their original decoration. The Jordan staircase is a magnificent white marble construction with gilt stucco and mirrors. On the first floor is the Armorial Hall, the largest room in the Winter Palace at 11,873 sq ft, its size making it ideal for large banquets and receptions. However, the most beautiful room in the palace is the Malachite Drawing Room designed by Alexander Brjullow in 1837 after the great fire.

Green malachite columns, gilded doors, decorated ceiling and capitals, deep red curtains and mirrors symbolize the splendor and magnificence of the

RIGHT
Pavilion hall in the
Little Hermitage ▶

FOLLOWING DOUBLE SPREAD
Winter Palace by
night ▶▶

◀ **LEFT**
The south facade of the
Winter Palace

tsars. The adjacent White Dining Room is particularly interesting because on the night of November 7, 1917, the Red Guards set up the civilian Provisional Government (which had forced Nicholas II to abdicate in March) here before Lenin took over government power.

Because of the enormous size of the Winter Palace, the tsars preferred living in their smaller summer residences, so that from the very beginning many of the rooms were used to exhibit their numerous art treasures. The collections of the Hermitage have been housed in the Winter Palace and the neighboring buildings (the Small Hermitage, the New Hermitage and the Great Hermitage) since 1917.

It is often difficult to say whether the magnificent rooms or the exhibits displayed in them are more impressive.

The Hermitage

The celebrated St Petersburg museum stands on a par with the Louvre in Paris, the British Museum in London and the Metropolitan Museum of Art in New York. Despite its 400 exhibition rooms, it has long been impossible to display all the objects in the Hermitage collection – there are 2.7 million of them! The former director of the museum, Piotrowski, has calculated that looking at each piece for only 30 seconds over an eight-hour-day, it would take over seven years to see them all.

How did so immense a collection come about? Peter I formed the basis of the collection with paintings and sculptures, and he arranged that it should receive all archaeological finds made in St Petersburg. His daughter Elisabeth I continued similarly, but the real art collector was Catherine the Great who bought 225 Dutch and Flemish masterpieces from a Berlin art dealer in the year 1764. This is taken as the year the Hermitage was founded. She took advantage of the financial problems of some European aristocrats and acquired a number of collections on favorable terms. After ten years, she already owned over 2,000 paintings. Alexander I and Nicholas I also added to the collection and it was opened to the public in the new Hermitage in 1852.

The collection experienced a considerable influx after the October Revolution because private collections were confiscated as "property of the people" and usually given to the Hermitage. Thus the museum's holdings quadrupled. A few years later, however a number of important works of art were sold to acquire much-needed foreign exchange.

Karlstein Castle

"I have just come from Karlstein. The Heiligkreuzkapelle (Holy Cross Chapel) in the large round tower, which used to house magnificent imperial insignia, contains the most remarkable expressions of religious splendor and art ... You have the impression that you have been transported into a magical world where all the colorful dreams of your childhood have become reality. You are looking at whole walls made from slabs of precious stones set in gold mortar, at a gold vault studded with precious stones, and at a number of paintings, mostly life-size, of most of the important saints in Christianity."

This enthusiastic description of the Holy Cross chapel by Sulpiz Boisserées is in no way exaggerated. It makes it clear that visitors to Prague should also go to Karlstein (22 miles south of the Czech capital) if they possibly can, so as not to miss an important artistic site. Karlstein Castle was declared a national heritage monument in 1964 and it is one of Bohemia's most important and beautiful fortresses.

It was built by Emperor Charles IV (1316–78) between 1348 and 1354 on top of a limestone hill nearly 1,000 ft high, as a safe place where he could house the coronation insignia and his valuable collection of holy relics. They remained there until the 15th century when they were moved to a supposedly safer place because of the Hussite wars. In retrospect this was unnecessary, because in 1422, the fortress survived a siege of seven months by the Hussites

without difficulty. In the 16th century, Karlstein was rebuilt in Renaissance style by Udalrico Avostalis, but 300 years later it was converted back to Gothic by the master cathedral builder Josef Mocker.

The fortress is built in terraces on the hilltop. It was originally approached by climbing slowly up the hill, each step taking the visitor further inside. At the same time, the views became better and the objects encountered increasingly valuable. Today, visitors no longer enter through the old fortress gate but through the gate of the Ursula Tower in the lower outer fortress. From there the route goes through a second fortress gate into the upper outer fortress. The fact that the inner fortress had two outer fortresses for increased security shows how important the emperor considered his treasures. He also laid the first stone of the fortress in a solemn ceremony unusual for the time.

Having finally reached the inner fortress through the main entrance, the next building is the imperial residence that contains collections related to the times, person and achievements of Charles IV. In the past, the stables were on the ground floor with the living quarters of the em-

FOLLOWING DOUBLE SPREAD
The Bohemian castle of Karlstein was besieged but never conquered ▶▶

◀ LEFT
The numerous stairways and terraces are quite tiring

peror's followers above. The two-aisled knights' hall with its coffered ceiling is supported by four wooden pillars. The private apartments of the Emperor Charles IV are on the top floor. The audience hall, the best-preserved room in the fortress, still has the original benches in the window recesses.

The Marian church with the Catherine chapel is situated in the neighboring Small Tower, also known as the Marian Tower. The frescoes date from the mid-14th century and were only rediscovered during Mocker's restoration work. They depict apocalyptic themes, and the Emperor as a collector of Christian relics. The altar recess has a painting depicting the Virgin Mary and the Infant Jesus with the Emperor Charles IV and his wife Anna von Schweidnitz. The ceiling is gilded as are the walls, which are also decorated with semi-precious stones. This priceless decoration is surpassed by the splendor of the Holy Cross Chapel in the large tower, as described by Sulpiz Boisserées. Between 2,300 and 2,500 precious stones such as jasper, amethyst, onyx and carnelian are set in gold. They vie for attention with 129 paintings on wood by Master Theodorich. The gilded ribbed vault, set with pieces of glass, looks like a sparkling starlit sky. Charles IV wanted only the best for his relics, something that would reflect their value. Although the portraits are attributed to the important Bohemian painter, it is quite obvious that some of the paintings are not by him – unsurprising in view of the large number of paintings. The coronation insignia and the relics are kept above the altar behind the gilded grille. Only a few chosen individuals were allowed to see these precious objects.

Emperor Charles IV – a real innovator

Charles IV was born in Prague in 1316 and brought up in Paris at the French court. Although he was already ruling Bohemia by 1342, he was not crowned king until 1347, a year after the death of his father Johann von Böhmen. He became Holy Roman Emperor in 1355.

Charles's main aim was to strengthen and expand his power base in Bohemia. Accordingly, he made Prague the center of his kingdom and strove to turn it into an important European city by erecting many new buildings. It is therefore no coincidence that many of its buildings have been named after him. As an intelligent, devout emperor he wanted to ensure lasting power not only on earth but also for eternity by his actions. He died in "his" city of Prague on 29 November 1378.

ROYAL PALACE, PRAGUE

As the center of important political events, the Old Royal Palace has a place not only in the history of Prague but also that of the world. It was here that the Second Defenestration of Prague took place in 1618, an event that triggered the Thirty Years War.

The Old Royal Palace is situated in the center of Prague Castle (see page 328) opposite the Golden Gate of Vitus' Cathedral. It was the seat of government of the Bohemian kings until the 16th century. In the 18th century, the palace became the seat of the central government office and was used for coronation festivities and for sessions of the provincial parliament. There are still some impressive remains of the old fortification walls under the present Royal Palace, dating from the 12th century when Sobeslav I started building it. Interrupted by a siege and a fire, the palace was finally completed by Vladislav II (1140–72). One hundred years later Otakar II decided it was necessary to "renovate" the palace. In 1252, he built a new residential wing in the west and later a transverse wing in the east. Charles IV also found it necessary to "renovate" the palace in 1345, as did Wenceslas IV (1361–1419). The residential quarters were constantly renewed and enlarged, but the most remarkable alterations were those carried out by Vladislav Jagiello in the 15th century.

The Vladislav Hall is arguably the most important secular expression of Gothic architecture north of the Alps. The size of the hall is immediately impressive; it is 203 ft long, 52 ft wide and 43 ft high. This is larger than a normal indoor riding school, so horse lovers may not be surprised to hear that equestrian events were held here. Because the hall is situated on the second floor, a special staircase was built with shallow but wide steps so that even horses could use it without harming their legs. It is known as the Riders' Staircase.

But the most remarkable feature of this hall is not so much its size as its ceiling. The vault, with its unique rib construction, covers the entire hall without any supporting columns in the middle. The elegant ribs spring from the inward-arching wall pillars, extending in graceful arches to the middle of the ceiling vault, where they meet in a star or flower shape to form five bays. The light, elegant lines of the ribs beautifully counteract the heavy, monumental impression of the hall. The large windows going down to the floor are no longer Gothic in style, but the first expression of the Renaissance north of the Alps.

The All Saints chapel, with its Renaissance doorway, abuts the

RIGHT
Ascent to the Vladislav Hall. Horses could be led up the Riders' Staircase with its wide, shallow steps to reach the Hall ▶

FOLLOWING DOUBLE SPREAD
View of Prague from the park of the Old Royal Palace ▶▶

◀ **LEFT**
Only after the fire in 1541 was the All Saints chapel integrated into the castle

Vladislav hall on the east side. It was consecrated as a royal chapel as early as 1185 and used to be separate from the castle. It was integrated after the fire that seriously damaged the castle in 1541.

A door in the north wall of the Vladislav Hall opens into the old Parliament Hall, built by Charles IV. When restoring the vault of the hall between 1559 and 1563 after the fire, Bonifaz Wolmut followed the original Gothic style of the ceiling but he built the head clerk's stand in Renaissance style. The royal throne at the front is more recent, dating from the 19th century. Until 1847, the Bohemian diet and regional court met here.

The new Land Statutes laid down after the fire were stored in the neighboring Land Chancery. It was in these books that all the important decisions and changes in Bohemia were recorded. Today, most of the Land Statute books are kept in the Central State archives.

A door in the southwest corner of the Vladislav Hall leads to the historic Louis wing, which was built by Benedikt Rieht between 1502 and 1509 in early Renaissance style. The greatest attraction in the palace, the Bohemian Chancery, situated in this part is where the Second Defenestration of Prague took place – from the east window to be precise. Two obelisks mark the place where the two governors are thought to have been thrown out of the window.

The Second Defenestration of Prague

During the reign of the Emperor Rudolf II (1552–1612), Prague flourished culturally but the seething conflict between Protestants and Catholics was intensifying. It was during this period that the Catholic League tried to break the Law of the Free Church, guaranteed by a royal decree. The Protestant representatives of the Diet called upon the people to protest against this. On 23 May 1618, a furious crowd stormed Prague Castle and the Royal Palace and threw the two governors of the Catholic party and a clerk out of the window. No one was seriously hurt – a heap of manure broke the fall – but this manifest escalation of the conflict between Catholics and Protestants was made worse by the monarch striving for greater power. This ultimately led to an uprising of the Diet, which finally turned into the Thirty Years War.

The First Defenestration of Prague had taken place in 1419 when an angry crowd threw the city councilors out of the town hall window onto spears placed below it because they refused to release supporters of the Reformation.

◀ **LEFT**
The Vladislav Hall with its remarkable rib vault was originally used for tournaments of knights

Prague Castle

It would be no exaggeration to call Prague Castle the largest fortress complex in the world. Its very varied elements include baileys and imposing buildings such as the Cathedral of St Vitus and the Golden Lane, making it very different from other European royal palaces. It is this very diversity of buildings and architectural styles that makes the Hradčany so fascinating.

By the end of the 9th century, the ruling house of the Premyslids had built a wooden fort on the left bank of the Vltava River, on a site that has remained important ever since. It was the nucleus around which Prague, the present capital of the Czech Republic, developed. Other buildings were built over the centuries including churches, the Royal Palace (see page 322), defense walls, peel towers and gardens. But it was only in the 18th century that the Hradčany acquired its presentday appearance, after Maria Theresa's project to extend the complex. Since 1918, it has also been the official residence of the President, whose presence is indicated by a white flag with the country's coat of arms and motto.

When climbing the sloping drive, visitors have a wonderful view of Prague with its rooftops and numerous towers, the surrounding hills and the statues of the fighting giants who guard the entrance of the castle. A gate with Rococo grilles leads to the main courtyard, the most recent part of the castle. The Rococo buildings, commissioned by Maria Theresa, were built between 1756 and 1774 under the supervision of Nikolaus von Pacassi.

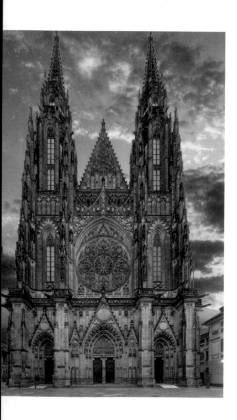

The Matthias Gate leading to the second courtyard was erected about 150 years earlier, and is the first Baroque building in Prague. Pacassi later incorporated it into his buildings. On the right is a staircase leading to the official state apartments of the president. The magnificent Spanish Hall and Rudolph's Gallery, both situated in the north wing of the second courtyard, are used for official receptions. In the center of the second courtyard, built in the first half of the 16th century, is a beautiful Baroque fountain by Francesco della Torre; it certainly outshines the other two fountains – the lion fountain and the draw-well.

The Holy Cross chapel that projects from the south wing in the second courtyard was built between 1758 and 1763 and is the oldest surviving chapel of the castle complex. It now houses a tourist information center. The undisputed focal point of the third courtyard is the famous cathedral of St Vitus. The tall, slender monolith next to the main entrance forms a strong contrast with the delicate facade. The sculpture by Josip Plecˇnik commemorates the victims of World War I. Nearby, an eques-

RIGHT
The church of St George is one of the best preserved buildings in Bohemia ▶

FOLLOWING DOUBLE SPREAD
The towers of the castle above the city of Prague with the Charles Bridge in the foreground ▶▶

◀ **LEFT**
The Heart of the Hradčany is the cathedral of St Vitus, built by Peter Parler, who was also involved in the building of Cologne cathedral

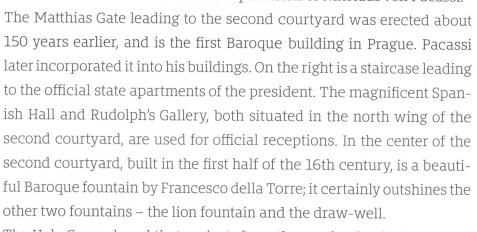

trian statue of St George fighting the dragon points towards the church of St George and its adjacent convent. It is the most important Romanesque building in Prague and is used for exhibitions organized by the national gallery and for concerts.

George Street leads to the east of the castle complex whose main attraction is the legendary Golden Lane. According to tradition, these tiny houses were inhabited by alchemists who produced gold in their workshops. The true tale is that the Emperor Rudolf II (1552–1612) installed the castle guards in these houses so that they would be close to their place of work. The pay was so bad that they also began to produce a few objects to sell, probably including some gold objects. It is plausible that guards would have been in the vicinity since the White and Daliborka Towers, the two defense towers along the north fortifications, were very close, flanking Golden Lane. They also served as a prison.

In the north of the Hradc̆any, across the Powder Bridge and the Deer Moat is the former riding school and a royal park. This is also where the most beautiful Renaissance building in Prague is to be found, the pleasure palace of Queen Anna. This building is known as the Belvedere by the inhabitants of Prague, because of its fine panoramic view. Designed by the Italian architect Paolo della Stella, it was built in 1538 and is surrounded by an open arcade. The upper floor is set back slightly, thus creating a flat ledge all around, resembling a balcony. Inside is a ballroom and gallery, as well as sumptuously furnished rooms. Sadly, these were plundered in the 17th century.

◄ **Left**
Today the magnificent Spanish Hall is used as a concert hall and for state receptions

St Vitus's Cathedral – one of the most important Gothic churches

Anyone who is reminded of Cologne's cathedral when looking at the cathedral of St Vitus should not be surprised – Peter Parler (1330/34–99) is known to have worked on both these 14th century buildings. In 1353, he took over the building of Prague cathedral and produced completely new architectural forms in the chancel, consecrated in 1385: the first monumental net vault and the earliest vesica piscis tracery. He also designed a wide range of architectural sculptures such as the 21 portrait busts on the Triforium. One of the busts is that of the master himself.

Parler was also responsible for the Golden Gate and the famous Wenceslas Chapel next to it. This chapel is the main attraction in the cathedral due to its rich decoration of precious stones. Built on the site of St Wenceslas's tomb, it contains wall paintings and a statue of the saint.

Castel del Monte

Castel del Monte sits on top of a hill like a large stone crown ruling the rolling countryside of the Murgia in Apulia. It is a symbol of worldly power that can be seen from far away, both terrifying and imposing at the same time. Its unusual octagonal shape makes it unlike any other castle or fortress, while adding a note of mystery and fascination.

This castle was built in about 1240 by the Hohenstaufen Holy Roman Emperor Frederick II, just returned from a crusade to Jerusalem and bursting with self-confidence, which was also reflected in the growing power of the empire. The architecture of the building was designed to reflect the emperor's background and character.

The octagonal building has eight octagonal towers linked by short wings of similar height, that form an octagonal inner courtyard. Seen from afar, the wide angles of the octagon appear rounded and seem to form a smooth circle. The projecting corner towers look like the points of a stone crown. From the outside, Castel del Monte looks closed in on itself and also cut off from the outside world: the massive towers do not look out onto the outside world with windows and doors, or even firing slits. They are completely isolated. The facades are smooth and undecorated, each wall only interrupted by two tiny windows, placed above each other. A stone stringcourse runs across the facades and towers halfway up the height of the building, holding them together like an iron band. This sober architecture makes the castle look impregnable and frightening, although it is not a fortress in the literal sense of the word. On the contrary, it was built as a residence, reflecting the owner's status.

Frederick loved grandeur and magnificence, and he decorated Castel del Monte in great splendor with marble walls and porphyry pilasters framing windows and doors. There were benches all round the walls of these high-ceilinged rooms and vast fireplaces providing welcome warmth. Water pipes and ventilation shafts passing through several floors ensured a degree of comfort rare in those days.

Because Castel del Monte was pillaged repeatedly during the centuries, not much has survived of that magnificent interior, but we can still imagine it. Visitors, historians and scholars of the esoteric try in vain to unravel the symbolic meaning of the octagonal structure. Links to holy towers, artistic and architectural traditions, or a connection between divine and earthly powers are some of the many theories advanced to explain the octagonal structure of Castel del Monte.

RIGHT
The entrance porch is the only decorated element on the exterior of Castel del Monte ▶

FOLLOWING DOUBLE SPREAD
The Hohenstaufen emperor Frederick II built Castel del Monte in the shape of a stone crown to demonstrate his power ▶▶

DOGE'S PALACE

The Palazzo Ducale or Doge's palace was both the headquarters and residence of the doge, the ruler of Venice. Situated on the east side of the Piazzetta San Marco, in the center of Venice, it is an outstanding expression of Venetian Gothic.

The Venetians moved to settle the group of islands around the Rialto in the 9th century. Already by this time, the doge's seat of government was housed in a well-fortified, wooden castle surrounded by canals. In the 14th century, it was replaced by an imposing, stone building. Building started in 1340 with the wing overlooking the pier that contains the great hall, known as the Sala dei Giganti. However, the Doge's Palace only acquired its present appearance over the course of the next three centuries; it was enlarged into a large palace with three wings to become a proud, imposing building that reflected the maritime and trading power of Venice.

The ground floor is bordered by an arcade of tall, pointed arches, giving the facade its characteristic look. The lively rhythm of the elegant columns with Gothic capitals, decorated with carved figures is repeated in the loggia above. But here they are more slender and delicate: one pointed arch on the ground floor corresponds to two Venetian-Gothic pierced arches in the loggia. The two were linked by a quatrefoil – a typical element of Gothic tracery – and in this way reflected the proportions and structure of the arcade on the ground floor. The loggia is not a projecting structure here as it is in many other buildings, and it forms a smooth facade with the ground floor and the floor above. The top floor is a blind wall, punctuated only by a few small windows. It is in striking contrast with the openness of the two floors below.

In spite of this, the effect of the facade is not overwhelming or oppressive. The marble decorative elements and the ornamental features along the roof reproduce the pointed arches effectively, softening the somber effect. The top floor with its distinctive pink and white pattern sparkles, as if covered by a silken veil.

Allegorical sculptures above the capitals of the columns ornament and emphasize the corners of the ducal palace. They depict "The Fall from Grace," "The Drunkenness of Noah" and "The

RIGHT
The "Porta della Carta" has one of the few windows on the top floor of the palace ▶

FOLLOWING DOUBLE SPREAD
View from the Canal di San Marco on Doge's Palace ▶▶

◀ **LEFT**
The loggia does not project beyond the ground floor but forms a flat facade unusual in Venice

Judgment of Solomon" and date from about 1400. The Doge's Palace housed the tribunal, the chancery and other administrative offices. It was also where the council met. The Palazzo Ducale was not only the seat of government, but also the doge's residence – he was generally only allowed to leave the palace for official functions. The magnificent architecture and decor of the Doge's Palace reflected its position as center of power of the thriving republic.

The beautiful facade with arcades was matched by an equally magnificent interior consisting of luxurious apartments with vast rooms and halls, as if to prove the equation: "Pomp plus splendor equals power." The Sala del Maggior Consiglio, the Hall of the Great Council, is breathtaking. It is 177 ft long and 82 ft wide, and is the largest medieval hall without supporting columns. In this impressive room, decorated with paintings exalting the Venetian Republic, 480 Venetian patricians (the figure later rose to 1,700) gathered to decide on matters concerning their city. Although the Hall dates from 1340 when the Palazzo was first built, the decoration was destroyed by a fire in 1577 and had to be completely restored. The central paintings on the ceiling depict the personification of Venice: Tintoretto shows Venice offering the Doge an olive branch.

In Vero nese's "Venice's Apotheosis," Venice is exalted not only by Venetians of all classes, but also by the allegories of Peace and Prosperity, to mention but two. At the front is the doge's throne with a painting by Tintoretto above it. Measuring 23 ft by 72 ft, it is the largest painting on canvas in the world.

The Sala del Collegio was where government decisions were made, officials welcomed and justice dispensed. The College, made up of ministers, councilors and members of the high court, sat on the rostrum with the doge and pronounced judgment. The votive picture above the doge's throne was painted by Veronese; the rest of the paintings of the doges are by Tintoretto.

The constitutional court and the Inquisition met in the Sala del Consiglio dei Dieci. The so-called Council of Ten dealt with cases of espionage and high treason as well as more minor crimes.

The Bridge of Sighs

Adjacent to the palace, but separated by a canal is the notorious prison. The palace is linked to it by a small, covered bridge. Having been sentenced in the Palazzo Ducale, prisoners crossed this bridge to be taken to the jail where they would serve their sentences. Looking out of the windows of the bridge, they would glance one last time at the beauty of the world outside, many of them sighing with despair as they did so. There is also a romantic legend associated with the bridge: when a couple kiss under the Bridge of Sighs, their love will last forever. Thus the bridge is known as the Bridge of Sighs or Ponte dei Sospiri, named for the sounds of despair or joy it inspires.

RIGHT
Doge's Palace interior ▶

◀ **LEFT**
Allegorical figures such as "Adam and Eve" ornament the corners of the Doge's Palace

Palazzo Medici-Riccardi

The Medici was Florence's most influential family – they were a successful banking dynasty as well as one of the most famous royal houses. They ruthlessly pursued their financial and political ends, but above all, they promoted the arts and were responsible for constructing the superb and exquisite architecture we associated with Florence today. The Palazzo Medici-Riccardi was the first residence and banking headquarters of the family and it became the architectural inspiration for many palazzos that followed it.

Palazzos in Florence developed from fortified castles into opulent residences with no defensive function. Originally an expression of the aristocracy's pride, palazzos began to play another role with the arrival of humanism, as architects built the urban palazzo to test and show off their talent. Michelozzo di Bartolomeo (1396–1472) who designed the Palazzo Medici-Riccardi was a predecessor of this new consciousness.

The massive, square building, taking up a whole street block, had a lasting influence on the design of subsequent Florentine palazzos. The elegant interior courtyard is like a secular version of a cloister and virtually became a standard feature of such buildings, together with the rustic facade reminiscent of a fortress. The emphasis on symmetry and balance, together with the expression of power, made rustic facades a status symbol in urban palaces. The huge classical cornice that surmounts the entire building was an innovative element that also influenced palazzo architecture.

Inside the palazzo is the Cappella dei Magi or Magi chapel, with its artistic masterpiece, the "Procession of the Three Kings" painted by Benozzo Gozzoli between 1459 and 1461. In it, the artist celebrates the Medici family in Gothic style. The procession is led by Lorenzo, followed by his grandfather, Cosimo the Elder, both on white horses customary for leaders.

In the mid-17th century, the Medici family became the royal ruling house. The palazzo that had been in the family for over two hundred years was sold since it no longer corresponded to their now more elevated status. The new owners were the Riccardi family, who enlarged the palazzo on the north side.

RIGHT
The elegant interior courtyard of the palazzo is reminiscent of a monastic cloister ▶

◀ **LEFT**
Part of the Mediterranean garden in the Florentine palazzo of the Medici

Palazzo Pitti

The Pitti Palace in Florence is one of the largest palaces in Italy, has some of the most beautiful gardens in the country and is one of the most important art galleries in the world.

Between 1457 and 1466, Luca Pitti, a merchant and friend of the Medici family, built a palace on the south bank of the Arno. He was forced to halt the building work after he had run out of money. For 80 years the palace remained unfinished until Eleonora of Toledo, the wife of Cosimo I, bought it in 1550. In 1560, she commissioned Bartolomeo Ammanati to rebuild and enlarge the palace. In 1565, Cosimo I moved out of the Palazzo Comunale (known today as the Palazzo Vecchio) and into the Pitti Palace with his family and court.

In 1620, the Pitti Palace was further enlarged under the supervision of Giulio Parigi. With its 650 ft facade, it was now the largest palace in the city. The Pitti Palace also housed the Medici picture gallery whose collections had been accessible to the public since 1640. The side wings were added in the 18th and 19th centuries. In the early 19th century, the little Meridiana palazzo was built at the back by the architect Pasquale Poccianti. Between 1865 and 1870, when Florence was the capital of Italy, the Pitti Palace became the king's residence. In 1919, King Victor Emmanuel III presented it as a gift to the Italian state.

The inner courtyard of the Pitti Palace leads to the Boboli gardens, created in 1560 by Cosimo I himself with the help of Niccolė Tribolo. The park contains some 200 statues as well as obelisks, fountains, grottoes, a theater and a cafe. Walking through the large gardens built on a hill slope, there is a magnificent view of the towers and rooftops of Florence. The exhibition rooms are approached from the inner courtyard. The extraordinary Pitti collections are all the more fascinating because of their setting in the sumptuous historical rooms of the Pitti Palace. There are many masterpieces including paintings by Titian and

RIGHT
The gallery in the largest palace in Florence has some of Titian and Raphael's most famous paintings ▶

◀ **LEFT**
Interior with numerous paintings and frescoes

Raphael, Rubens, Tintoretto, van Dyck, Velazquez, Murillo, Caravaggio, Giorgione, Perugino and Filippo Lippi.

The Museo degli Argenti contains some superb craft objects that once belonged to the Medici. The Appartamenti Monumentali were the residential quarters and official state rooms of the Tuscan archdukes and Italian kings and they have been left in their original condition. The Galleria d'Arte Moderna is only "modern" by comparison to the majority of Florentine art, because it's paintings date from the 19th century.

Castello Sant'Angelo

Steep walls built from giant square blocks of stones form the basis of this monumental bastion. It was not built to guarantee the safety of the living, but to house the dead. This impressive building was originally built as a mausoleum for Emperor Hadrian. It later became a fortress and is a museum today.

Emperor Hadrian erected this circular building on the right bank of the Tiber in the center of Rome between 135 and 139 AD. He was probably inspired by the mausoleum of Augustus, situated nearby. In the third century, Emperor Aurelius integrated this mighty mausoleum into the town walls and used it as fortress.

In 590, the plague raged in Rome and killed hundreds of people. Doctors were at their wit's end and praying seemed to be the only course to follow. Pope Gregory the Great organized a procession through Rome with people praying to the Almighty, asking him to bring an end to the pestilence. When the procession reached Hadrian's mausoleum at the town walls, Gregory had a vision of the archangel Michael on the top of the fort. The archangel slipped his sword back into his sheath, as a sign that the plague would soon come to an end. The building's name, Castel Sant'Angelo (Castle of the Angel), was inspired by this legend. At the beginning of the seventh century under Pope Boniface, a chapel dedicated to St Michael was built on top of the fort and crowned by a statue of the angel. Hadrian's mausoleum became a real fortress at the turn of the first millennium.

During the centuries that followed, many popes took refuge in Castel Sant'Angelo. Indeed, in 1277, Pope Nicholas II built a secret underground passage linking the palace of the Vatican to Castel Sant'Angelo. The Renaissance popes Alexander VI and Julius II designed the luxurious interior decor. Their zest for life is clearly reflected in the painted ceilings, alive with sensual putti and other naked figures. The bath commissioned by Pope Clement VII from Giulio Romano (a pupil of Raphael) was small but lavishly decorated with stucco and grotesques. There are 58 rooms in the Museum Castel Sant'Angelo and a panoramic view of Rome from the top of the fort. The exhibits include models of buildings, weapons and a treasury. The Ponte Sant'Angelo, whose central arcades are part of the original bridge of 135 AD, links Castel Sant'Angelo to the other bank of the Tiber. The ten statues of angels on the bridge are by Gian Lorenzo Bernini, Rome's genius of Baroque sculpture.

RIGHT
The road to Castel Sant'Angelo crosses the Ponte Sant'Angelo, which, like the fort itself, is adorned with statues of angels ▶

◀ **LEFT**
Statue of Archangel Michael

Castello Sforzesco

From fortress to residence, garrison and finally museum – the Castello Sforzesco in Milan has had many functions in its checkered history as a secular building belonging to the European aristocracy.

In 1368, the Visconti family built a square fortress with four corner towers in the northwest quarter of Milan. However, after the death of Filippo Maria Visconti in 1447, the fortress was pillaged and destroyed. Francesco Sforza married the daughter of the last Visconti duke, and rebuilt the fortress on the same site in 1450. At first, Sforza was mainly interested in the defensive features of the new Castello, and so he commissioned the military architects Marcoleone da Nogarolo and Filippo di Ancona to design the plans for the new building. The two architects made use of the defensive ground plan of the original castle, and built a citadel in the northwest – the Rochetta. Bartolomeo Gadio was responsible for the two massive, compact, round towers with their decorative lozenge pattern, built in 1459. They flank the two southern wings on the corners and the dominating Torre del Filarete. The striking Torre del Filarete, built in 1451, reaches a height of 230 ft and is topped with battlements. It is named after its architect.

Sforza's son, Galeazzo Maria, built the Corte Ducale and converted other buildings into a residence near the Rochetta, decorating them with paintings. He moved there with his court from the Palazzo di Corte near the cathedral. Under Ludovico il Moro and his art-loving wife Beatrice d'Este, Milan flourished as the cultural center of Italy. This was also reflected in the Castello Sforzesco: Donato Bramante built the entrance portal and a covered bridge, while Leonardo da Vinci decorated several rooms with paintings.

When the Spanish conquered Milan in 1535, they converted Castello Sforzesco to its original use as a fortress. They turned the residence into one of Europe's largest garrisons, housing some 3,000 soldiers and surrounding it with six star-shaped bastions. These bastions were demolished at the end of the 18th century after Milan's conquest by the French in 1796 and no trace of them can be seen today.

As time went by Castello Sforzesco fell into disrepair because it was no longer used. Eventually it was restored by Luca Beltrami at the end of the 19th century. It was seriously damaged in World War II, has been rebuilt and restored. The Corte Ducale is now the Musei del Castello Sforzesco, which contains the city's art collections of important paintings by old masters and sculptures. There is also a museum of musical instruments.

Right
The Torre del Filarete,
the gate tower of the
Castello Sforzesco ▶

STUPINIGI

The concept of European Baroque art has rarely been so carefully worked out and expressed as forcefully as in the hunting lodge of Stupinigi, whose individual architectural style clearly sets it apart from all other Baroque castles. In the Stupinigi hunting lodge, sculpture, painting and garden design have been combined to create a harmonious ensemble.

Although (or perhaps because) the region of Savoy and Piedmont was constantly threatened by France and Spain, 17th century Turin was surrounded by a series of castles built by the House of Savoy as an expression of its sovereignty. In 1713, Duke Vittorio Amedeo II of Savoy also became King of Sicily, so that the sphere of influence of the House of Savoy became even wider and its position of power greater. In the years that followed, the king commissioned the Sicilian architect Filippo Juvarra to turn the castles near Turin into monumental residences befitting an absolute monarch. In 1729, he decided that he also needed a hunting lodge to reflect his status.

Juvarra had already worked in Rome, Lisbon and Madrid and was internationally renowned. He had excellent qualifications for the task because he inspired the trust of his client, he had great experience, he knew the skills of his craftsmen, and if necessary, he could attract artists from afar. He had an ideal site that did not restrict his plans in spite of local topography or the existence of other buildings. As a result, he created an ensemble in which the landscape, garden and buildings are connected by several axes intersecting at the hunting lodge at the center. Juvarra proved himself an excellent architect of Baroque art, involving himself in everything from the overall planning stage to the more detailed plans, the actual construction and the interior decoration. In other words, Juvarra was involved in every detail concerning the building of the hunting lodge. It was to be his last work in the region of Turin.

The tall central building that contains the ballroom is situated in the center, at the intersection of the various axes. It is surmounted by a cupola with a bronze deer on top, to remind visitors of its function as a hunting lodge. The four wings are arranged in an X-shape around the oval central building. As a result, the main axis of the castle is at a right angle to the drive leading to Turin. The front residential wings are further extended by side wings and annexes containing the living apartments and farm

RIGHT
The round, arched doors lead from the park directly into the ballroom ▶

FOLLOWING DOUBLE SPREAD
Four residential wings are arranged around the oval central building. The main axis of the hunting lodge is therefore at right angles to the avenue leading to Turin ▶▶

◀ **LEFT**
The frescoes of hunting scenes decorating the walls and ceilings reflect Stupinigi's function as a hunting lodge

buildings. The axes formed by the individual wings are extended beyond the castle in the form of avenues and paths leading to the hunting grounds in the forest.

The facades of all the buildings are homogeneous in design but with increasing ornamentation towards the central building. The pilasters emphasize the verticality, as do the tall, symmetrically-arranged windows of the main floor. A balustrade visually links the round cupola with the flat roofs of the wings, which all vary in height. Vases and hunting trophies ornament the balustrade along the central building.

The shallow steps leading to the ballroom are also decorated with a balustrade. Three large French windows, surmounted by round arches whose shape is repeated in the windows of the second floor, open onto this vast hall, which is the height of two floors. Opposite are the round, arched doors leading into the garden. Like the French windows of the main entrance, they make the greenery of the garden part of the room, almost integrating it into the design, thus creating a harmonious link between indoors and out.

Four free-standing pillars support the central cupola and the four outward-curving flattened domes of the oval ballroom. A gallery runs around the whole room, halfway up. Juvarra commissioned the brothers Domenico and Giuseppe Valeriani of Venice to decorate the walls and ceiling. The magnificent fresco decorating the main cupola depicts "the goddess Diana hunting" – it is perfectly suited to a hunting lodge.

The apartments of the king and queen are located in the two residential wings overlooking the garden. They too were magnificently decorated in splendid Rococo style under Juvarra's supervision, and he chose all the artists himself. The interior decoration and furniture have survived almost intact – only a few pieces have had to be replaced. The replacement furniture all came from other castles belonging to the House of Savoy.

From Stupinigi to the Palazzo Reale

An avenue 6 miles long used to lead from the main courtyard of the Stupinigi to the Porta Nuova in Turin. Beyond it, this avenue continued to the royal palace, the Palazzo Reale. (Today the avenue is a multi-lane main road.) The Palazzo Reale is a rather plain building that was built in the 17th century. Its sumptuously decorated rooms contrast strongly with its rather sober exterior. The royal library contains drawings by Leonardo da Vinci, Raphael and Rembrandt. King Carlos Alberto declared war against Austria from the balcony of the Palazzo Reale in March 1848.

ROYAL PALACE, MONACO

For many people, Monaco conjures up images of a tax haven, casinos and Formula 1 motor racing. It is the palace of the reigning Grimaldi family, Prince Rainier and the princesses Caroline and Stephanie. It evokes memories of the unforgettable Grace Kelly, the American actress who captured the heart of a prince.

The story of Monaco started in the 13th century when Fulco del Cassello laid the first stone of a castle in 1215, on the site of the present palace. Francesco Grimaldi arrived in 1297, disguised as a monk, having been expelled from Genoa. He succeeded in capturing the fortress that has been associated with the Grimaldi family ever since. In 1454, the Grimaldis grabbed power from the Genoese, who had secured a foothold here in the Middle Ages. Since then, the Grimaldi dynasty, the oldest ruling dynasty in Europe, has succeeded in maintaining the independence of its small kingdom, albeit with a few interruptions.

In the first half of the 17th century, Honoré II substantially enlarged the Renaissance palace by adding the right wing with the Grands Apartments. He collected many valuable treasures, from furniture to paintings and silver. During his lifetime, the collection grew to 700 items.

The palace is situated in an elegant district of the city of Monaco. When the flag is hoisted on the roof it means that Prince Albert II is in residence. He is the son of Rainier III, who surprised the world in 1956 by marrying the American actress Grace Kelly. She had starred in three Hitchcock films as the "blond ice-maiden." As Princess Grace, she won everyone's heart but died tragically in a car accident in 1982.

One of the wings of the palace is a museum while the Grimaldis live in the southwest wing. Parts of the private apartments can be visited in summer when the royal family leaves the hot Mediterranean for cooler climes. However, it is possible to see the members of the Grimaldi family at any time – in the wax museum of the royal family.

RIGHT
13th century ancestor of the royal family Francesco Grimaldi statue ▶

FOLLOWING DOUBLE SPREAD
The Royal Palace of the Grimaldi family is inhabited by Prince Albert II and his family, and it also contains a museum ▶▶

◀ **LEFT**
Monaco coat of arms

ALHAMBRA

The Arab poet Ibn Zamrak expressed his admiration for the Alhambra by declaring, " The stars themselves would stay with her instead of endlessly moving around the sky." This fairy tale Eastern castle, which dominates the Spanish town of Granada in Andalusia it is both a fortress and a castle, a most beautiful expression of Islamic architecture in Spain.

The Alhambra is particularly impressive when the sun sets against the grandiose background of the Sierra Nevada and the ocher-red stones shimmer in the red light of dusk. The castle lives up to its name because "al-Hambra" means "the Red." Red was also the color of the Nasrids, a Spanish-Arab dynasty, so the name of the fortress could also refer to the founder of the Alhambra. It was the Nasrid ruler Mohammed I who extended the oldest part, the Alcazaba, in 1238. Subsequent Moorish kings of Spain continued to enlarge the fortress between the 13th and 15th centuries and built the actual core of the fortress complex, the Alhambra itself. The third part is the palace built by Emperor Charles V directly next to the Arab royal palace, the Palacio Arabe.

The city of Granada, the fertile high plateau and the surrounding hills were best controlled from the rocky foothills of the Sierra Nevada and the Zirids had already erected a fortress there. Mohammed I enlarged it, adding a double row of fortification walls and several towers to the Alcazaba. Tapering to a point and adapted to the topography of the hill, it is the oldest part, west of the Alhambra. The Alcazaba served purely military purposes until Mohammed I decided to move his residence here and built the Alhambra to live and rule from. The square building with a solid, undecorated facade with few windows has a severe, uninviting appearance giving no hint of the magnificence of the interior.

The Palacio Arabe was not built to a strict design, but follows the usual plan of a Moorish house whose rooms open onto a square inner court. This arrangement is repeated over and over again with the result that the rooms and courts are so interconnected that they form a real labyrinth. Nevertheless, three main areas are distinguished: the Cuarto Dorado (Golden Court) with the Mexuar where justice was administered, the Cuarto de Comares or Diwan where official receptions were held, and the Cuarto de los Leones (Lion Court) or Harim which contained the private quarters.

RIGHT
Tower of Justice on the southern rampart of the fortress ▶

FOLLOWING DOUBLE SPREAD
This unique expression of Moorish architecture and power is set against the beautiful background of the snow-covered Sierra Nevada mountains ▶▶

◀ **LEFT**
Cupola in the Hall of the Two Ladies, encrusted with sparkling decoration

◀ **LEFT**
The summer palace of the Generalife has beautiful formal gardens with fountains and water, like the Patio de Acequia shown here

The Mexuar is the oldest part of the palace. Justice was administered in this audience chamber and it later became the seat of government. Its walls were embellished with Moorish decorations, and it was subsequently used as a chapel. The Mexuar is second only to the Cuarto Dorado with its gilt stucco walls and calligraphic friezes. The left door leads to the heart of the Alhambra, the Patio de los Arrayanes or Myrtle Court. A large, rectangular fishpond, surrounded by a myrtle hedge, dominates the court. The short sides of the rectangle are bordered with elegant, slender arcades which are beautifully reflected in the water.

The Torre de Comares opposite is the tallest part of the complex at 148 ft. It includes the Sultan's apartments: a remarkable reception room decorated with numerous Arabic verses in stucco, most of which were written by Ibn Zamrak who naturally also included the palace and its founder in his praises. The walls of the Throne Room are decorated with colorful stoneware and stucco: arabesques, Kufic letters (that is characters in the monumental square Arabic script), suras from the Koran and poetic verses.

The ceiling consists of a wooden dome symbolizing the seven heavens of the Muslims and the stars in the firmament. The Lions' Court is in the private quarters of the palace. The four small water channels symbolizing the four rivers of paradise divide the court into four areas. They meet at the Lion Fountain, a basin of water supported by twelve lions representing the sun and the signs of the zodiac. The court is surrounded by arcades with elegant columns with Nasridic capitals, all 124 of them different from each other. To the east of the court is the King's Hall whose ceiling is decorated with paintings of playing and hunting scenes, depicting the rulers of the House of Nasrids. They are painted on leather, and are very unusual for Moorish art because pictures and images are forbidden by the Koran. The Hall of the Two Sisters, situated to the north, is a high point of Moorish architecture. It takes its name from the two large marble slabs in the floor. The ceiling consists of a Mukarna or stalactite-cupola encrusted with mocarabes (pointed plasterwork that creates the effect of a star) sparkling over the sultana and her children who lived here.

To the south of the palace is the palace built by Charles V, an imposing square Renaissance building which presents a stark contrast to the splendor of the Arabian parts. It has a round interior courtyard surrounded by superimposed arcades, and is reminiscent of a bullfighting arena. In 1526, Pedro Machuca incorporated it into the Alhambra fortress.

The Generalife

The summer palace of the Nasrids stands on the Cerro del Sol above the Alhambra. It was completed in 1319, and contains a delightful enclosed Moorish garden with fountains. A path leads from the Alhambra to the Patio de Acequia with its long, narrow water channel and many jets. At the north and south ends of the garden are pavilions with columns and stucco decoration.

RIGHT
Palace of Charles V dating from the 16th century, now the National Museum of Spanish-Islamic Art ▶

FOLLOWING PAGE
View of the famous Lion Fountain, with the water basin and twelve lions symbolizing the sun and the signs of the zodiac ▶▶

PAGE AFTER NEXT
Superb wall decoration in the Patio del Mexuar, the oldest part of the Alhambra ▶▶▶

ROYAL PALACE, ARANJUEZ

"The beautiful days of Aranjuez have now drawn to a close." This is how Friedrich Schiller started his play "Don Carlos," and gave Aranjuez a place in world literature. Those who know this charming castle of the Habsburgs and Bourbons will understand the feeling of nostalgia contained in these words.

The city of Aranjuez is built along the Tagus about 31 miles south of the Spanish capital Madrid. The fertile valley surrounding the city produces asparagus, strawberries, flowers, trees and bushes, so that Aranjuez is like an oasis in the Meseta – the barren center of Spain. It was this particularly beautiful valley that persuaded King Philip II to build the summer residence of the royal family here. In 1569, his architect Juan de Herrera, also involved in building El Escorial (see page 380), produced the plans for the conversion of the house-palace of the Master of Santiago Order, built in 1387. The castle was only completed two centuries later in 1778, and its cheerfully charming appearance is in pleasing contrast to the sober austerity of the Escorial. It was a pleasant place where the royal family could relax and dream. The strong impression of warmth is created to a large extent by the building material. Herrera chose a warm shade of light reddish-brown for the bricks and pale limestone for the window frames, pilasters and other decoration, thus creating a lively contrast in the facade. This contrast was coupled with the rhythmic design of the facade and retained by both owners and architects throughout the long building period, so that the two-storied palace with its square inner courtyard produces a very harmonious appearance.

The facade as it is today was designed by the Italian Giacomo Bonavia. After studying Herrera's plans, he gave the central part more prominence by building a staggered roof line in 1748. The roof is adorned with a balustrade and the part above the entrance is further ornamented with sculptures of the most important royal owners of the palace, Philip

RIGHT
The alternation of pale reddish-brown bricks and light sandstone gives the castle a lively appearance ▶

FOLLOWING DOUBLE SPREAD
Since 1779, summer garden parties for which special open air music for wind instruments was composed have been regularly organized ▶▶

◀ **LEFT**
Sculptures of heroes and gods of antiquity adorn the park of Aranjuez

II (1556–98), Philip V (1683–1746) and Ferdinand VI (1713–59).

Charles III (1716–88) also wanted to alter and enlarge the castle. He asked the Italian architect Francesco Sabatini to build the side wings, probably inspired by the Baroque residences of many parts of Europe. This was to be the last addition to the building. The Bourbons of the 18th and 19th century decorated the castle according to the fashion of the day, so the rooms on the top floor are furnished either in Moorish, Chinese or Pompeian style. The Porcelain Room of Charles III, created by Giuseppe Cricci and his Neapolitan craftsmen over the course of six years (1759–65), is particularly splendid.

Charles V (1500–58) created a forest-like park in the 16th century, importing elms and other trees from England. It was the first large landscaped park in Spain. There were also flower gardens in the old house-palace of the Master of the Order of Santiago. These were gradually altered by subsequent occupants of the castle. In the 17th century, the Italian garden architect Cosimo Lotti created the Jardín de Isla, a park with ponds, fountains, flower borders and sculptures of the gods and heroes of antiquity, as was the current European Baroque fashion. In 1780, Charles IV redesigned the Jardín del Principe according to his taste. Today the Marine Museum is situated in this park. The museum contains restored royal barges on which the king and his court used to enjoy elegant feasts while the boats glided slowly on the Tagus.

The Casa del Labrador

To the northeast of Aranjuez is the Casa del Labrador. This small castle was built on the site of a farmhouse, which gave the castle its name. (There is an illustration of it in the cellar of the palace.) Charles IV discovered this quiet, secluded spot while hunting and built this latest Bourbon castle between 1792 and 1803. The historic architecture and lavish Rococo decoration in keeping with the period give the Casa del Labrador a particularly elegant appearance.

Queen María Luisa and her lover met here in these sumptuous rooms. He was the important government minister Mañuel Godoy. After Godoy formed an alliance with France, Spain fought many battles with Great Britain and Portugal, incurring heavy losses. This led to an increasing dependence on France. In the spring of 1808, dissatisfaction hed to revolt in Aranjuez. Charles IV was forced to abdicate and the Francophile Godoy was driven out – out of office and out of the Casa del Labrador.

Coca Castle

One thousand and one nights in Spain: Coca Castle is one of the most beautiful fortresses in Spain and a magnificent example of Mudéjar architecture.

This jewel of fortress architecture lies west of the town of Coca, some 31 miles from Segovia. Because the castle is made of red bricks, it appears to shimmer with warm shades of red. This agreeable appearance is further enhanced by the many turrets that add a playful note and counteract the monolithic fortified aspect of the fortress.

Like many others, Don Alfonso de Fonseca, Archbishop of Seville, wanted an imposing castle appropriate to his social position which could double as a mighty fortress. He was fond of splendor and magnificence, but he was a key figure at court who enjoyed palace intrigues and had many enemies. Indeed, in the 15th century when he built the fortress, the threat in central Spain did not come from the Moors – the religious war was over – but from personal enemies or rival aristocratic families.

Surrounded by fortified walls with massive, bulky watchtowers, Coca Castle is extremely well-protected. The walls of the fortifications and of the castle itself are embellished with decorative windows. The walls, gates and towers are in the Mudéjar style combining Islamic and Christian (especially Gothic) architectural features. These include decorative stucco and strapwork as well as Moorish horseshoe arches that were added to the walls of the keep to form a pointed arch.

RIGHT
The decorative character of the towers contrasts with the otherwise massive nature of the fortress castle ▶

◀ **LEFT**
The inhabitants of Coca Castle were well protected against the Moors and rival aristocratic families

El Escorial

The "budding" Baroque of El Escorial in Spain is as important architecturally as the Palace of Versailles in France. The Escorial is a perfect example of early Baroque architecture while the combination of convent, church and residence represents the close link between the church and the monarchy that existed in 16th century Spain.

It was on the feast of St Lawrence in the year 1557 that King Philip II of Spain (who ruled 1556–98) won his victory over the French. To give thanks for God's divine support, the deeply religious king built "El Real Monasterio de San Lorenzo de El Escorial" some 31 miles south of Madrid. He carefully selected the raised site on the slopes of the Guadarrama Mountains and supervised the building works from 1572 to 1584. He commissioned Juan Bautista Toledo and the Italian architect Giambattista Castello (who worked with Michelangelo on the Vatican) to produce plans. Juan Herrera took over after Toledo's death, further developing the somber style of the Escorial.

The almost square ground plan of the Escorial, with its 650 ft sides, is subdivided into almost square units to produce a grid effect, a reference to the gridiron on which St Lawrence was burnt alive. The facades themselves are punctuated by numerous small windows, placed at regular intervals so that they too create a grid effect. Four square corner towers on the outer wings give the building the forbidding appearance of a fortress. Two taller square bell-towers next to the entrance to the basilica and the vast dome above the church convey the concept that the religious nature of the complex is more important than the secular. Moreover, the basilica is not only the tallest, but the also the largest building in the Escorial. To the north is the Palacio Real (Royal Palace), situated next to the church. The palace is adjacent to the basilica and evidently much smaller, so it looks like an annexe and symbolizes the fact that Philip II saw his buildings as an offering to God. His apartments are modest and relatively small, next to the church and looking out far over the plain. From his simple room containing a bed and a worktable, he ruled over his empire. The furnishing of the king's small apartment is in striking contrast to the Bourbon rulers who came after him. The Bourbon apartments, decorated with paintings by Goya and Rubens, are more impressive.

Philip's desire to see the main altar from his bedroom shows his almost fanatical religious zeal. This exaggerated religious fervor was also reflected by the fact that the monks of the Escorial monastery prayed uninterruptedly for the salvation of the royal family and for the souls of all the Spanish

Right
The vast chancel of the almost windowless church emphasises the nothingness of earthly existence ▶

Following double spread
The basilica, royal palace, monastery and mausoleum are all housed in one complex, the Escorial ▶▶

◀ **Left**
"The Pantheon of the Kings" contains the mortal remains of the Spanish Habsburg kings

kings of the Habsburg and Bourbon royal houses laid to rest in the mausoleum of the Escorial (apart from of Philip V and Ferdinand VI who were buried elsewhere).

The main entrance portal, embellished by superimposed columns, is decorated with a statue of St Lawrence with the royal coat-of-arms underneath. The porch opens onto the Patio de los Reyes (Courtyard of the Kings), which is flanked by the monastery seminary on the left and by the library on the right. However, the most striking building is the monastery church, built by Toledo and clearly inspired by St Peter's Basilica in Rome. The building consists of a central section with a cupola 295 ft high over the crossing. Built mostly in plain gray granite, only the chancel is decorated with gold, bronze, marble and didactic panel paintings. Under the main chapel is the royal crypt. Ordinary people are not allowed to worship in this main church but only in the ante-church, situated in front of the main church where the ground plan of the central church is repeated in the space between the bell-towers.

To the south of the church is the Courtyard of the Evangelists, named after the statues of the evangelists that decorate the pump-room. It is surrounded by the sacristy, the chapter rooms and the old church. The chapter rooms, whose major paintings are now on display in the Prado in Madrid, still contain magnificent treasures including works by El Greco, Velázquez, Tintoretto, Titian and Veronese. At the time some 200 monks lived in the monastery, which had a library of 40,000 books and manuscripts covering all areas of knowledge in the 16th century. The books and manuscripts are arranged in wonderful bookcases of fine wood. They are arranged not with their spines facing outward as they would be nowadays, but with the gilt edging towards the room so that they could breathe. The atmosphere of learning emanating from this library, one of the finest in Europe, is enhanced by frescoes on the walls and the vaulted ceiling. The frescoes were painted by Pellegrino Tibaldi, and depict allegories of philosophy, theology, grammar, rhetoric, geometry, music and astronomy.

The remains of the kings

According to the wishes of Philip II, the Escorial was also to serve as a mausoleum for the Spanish kings. The remains of nearly all Habsburg and Bourbon rulers were moved from all over the country to the Escorial. Don Juan of Austria's body was brought here from The Netherlands. Because the body had to pass through the unfriendly territory of France, it was divided into three parts and carried in saddlebags in order to be as inconspicuous as possible.

CASTLE OF LOARRE

This striking fortress-monastery rises high above the barren landscape of the lonely plain near the Franco-Spanish border, and is a reminder of the uncertain times when Christians and Moors vied for supremacy in Spain.

The Castillo de Loarre is hardly visible from the distance, but as one approaches, the castle seems to emerge from the rocks. It was built on the site of an ancient Iberian fort, erected to secure the safety of the surroundings. In the 10th century, the present complex was already an important bulwark against the Moors and therefore one of the oldest fortresses in Spain. It fell to the Moors in 1065, but the castle was recaptured very soon afterwards. It was enlarged and further fortified so that it would not be captured again, and a monastery and chapel were built within the defensive fortifications.

This fortress chapel is constructed on a slope. On the side facing the slope, it has only two stories, but there are three on the outside. The outside facade, is decorated with horizontal friezes with a check pattern that marks the height of the different floors. The windows are framed by columns and above the entrance porch is a representation of the Last Judgment, of which, unfortunately, only the lower half survives. The apse is detached from the main nave of the chapel, and is framed by half-columns and wall arches.

The fortress was the favorite residence of the kings of Aragon. The kingdom flourished and Loarre became a thriving center. The wall paintings and remains of reliefs recently discovered in the so-called "apartment of the queen" reflect the important part then played by the castle. But this fame did not last because King Sancho I Ramirez founded another fortress-monastery in Montearagón and moved the monks from Loarre to this new establishment.

The vast fortifications with ten watchtowers, the keep, residential quarters and chapel were all built in the 13th century. But when the Spanish reconquered the Iberian peninsula, the need for defense in the region ended and the castle of Loarre lost much of its importance.

RIGHT
The fortress-monastery of Loarre was an island of Christianity in Moorish-occupied country ▶

FOLLOWING DOUBLE SPREAD
Visible from afar, the fortress rises high above the beautiful plain of Aragon ▶▶

◀ **LEFT**
Capital in Castle Loarre

Royal Palace, Madrid

When the national flag flies on the royal palace in Madrid it means that the King of Spain is in the palace and probably receiving important guests. This imposing Baroque palace is no longer used as a royal residence, but only for official events and receptions.

Very important visitors are received with great ceremony on the parade ground, situated between the cathedral (only completed in 1993) and the Royal Palace. The palace was built between 1737 and 1764 to the plans of the Italian architect Giovanni Battista Sacchetti. A new palace was needed because the old Alcázar was destroyed in a fire three years before.

The new palace was built on the same site, on a hill overlooking the Sierra Guadarrama. Built on a square ground plan like the old fortress, it consists of four wings around an internal courtyard. Each wing has a central and two corner projections, and is divided visually into two, using dark stones that give the appearance of a plinth along the base of the building. The palace looks imposing and majestic with its 500 ft facade, relatively unadorned and punctuated only by pilasters. The impression is softened by the decorative roof balustrade, which is embellished with statues and vases. Above the entrance portal is a very ornate superstructure with a large clock.

Several artists were responsible for the sumptuous interior decoration of the palace, including the German painter Anton Raphael Mengs who came to Madrid as a court painter, and the celebrated Venetian painter Giovanni Battista Tiepolo, who painted the "Apotheosis of the Spanish Monarchy" in the Small Audience Chamber next to the Throne Room. His ceiling frescoes are impressive – not only due to their brilliant combination of colors, but also because the viewpoint of the observer is always taken into account.

The interior decoration of the private apartments dates from the 19th and 20th century. The Royal Dispensary has a collection of instruments dating from the 17th to the 20th century, giving visitors an insight into the medicine and pharmaceutical remedies of the past. The Royal Library consists of 24 rooms with over 300,000 books, other printed matter, manuscripts and maps. It also includes musical instruments and a collection of coins.

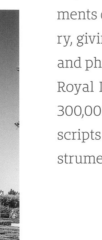

RIGHT
The Small Audience Chamber contains Tiepolo's fresco, "The Apotheosis of the Spanish monarchy" ▶

FOLLOWING DOUBLE SPREAD
Important guests are welcomed on the parade ground ▶▶

NEXT DOUBLE SPREAD
The Throne Room decorated in magnificent baroque style with frescoes by Tiepolo contrasts strongly with the restraint of the exterior facade ▶▶▶

◀ **LEFT**
The palace is set in a simple garden with carefully pruned trees and hedges

Peñafiel Castle

The fortress is built on a mountain ridge and seems to have grown out of the rock. The towers and walls are the same pale color as the rocks, as if a giant had carved them from the landscape.

Peéafiel Castle, one of the most impressive fortresses in Castile, rises high above the Rio Duero in central Spain. For centuries it was used by both the Christians and the Moors to protect the border. It acquired its present name in the 11th century. After King Sancho had recaptured it from the Arabs, he is said to have thrust his sword into the ground and cried out "From today onward this fortress is the true (fiel) rock (peÈa) of Castile." In the 15th century, the members of the Calatrava order built the present fortress on the ruins of this early Romanesque fort.

The castle of Peéafiel is 690 ft long but only 75 ft wide, tapering even more at the extremities. The thirty towers with battlements enabled the guards to detect enemies or potential attackers from a great distance so that they could prepare their defense. Should the enemy succeed in climbing to the top of the hill, there was still a double row of defense walls for them to overcome in their exhausted state.

There is a wonderful view of the surroundings from the residential quarters in the tower, which King Alfonso X (1221–84) must also have enjoyed when he lived there. This king was an intellectual, known as "el sabio" ("the wise") and he retained the name given to the castle by his predecessor because he encouraged the development of universities and the propagation of the Castilian language. In addition, he supported the making of legal digests, and the compilation of histories of Spain and of the world, although these were never completed. The king was a writer himself and is credited with making the Castilian language the common language of Spain.

The town of Penafiel

Today the fortress overlooks a peaceful Castilian town. The central square where all festivities take place dates from the Middle Ages, but the surrounding twostoried houses are more recent, dating from the 18th century. The church of San Pablo dating from 1324 has a magnificent apse with decorated horseshoe and pointed arches.

RIGHT
King Alfonso X, champion of the Castilian tongue, lived in the residential tower of Peñafiel Castle ▶

FOLLOWING DOUBLE SPREAD
This forbidding fortress rising above the Rio Duero frightened off potential enemies ▶▶

Peñíscola Castle

The imposing Templar fortress of Peñíscola is situated to the north of Valencia on the Costa del Azahar. Its unique location – in the mountains on a thin rocky outcrop 210 ft above the sea – has ensured its place in the history of Christianity, since it was used as a refuge by the antipope Benedict XIII.

Peníscola Castle is made up of three distinct parts. The oldest dates from the 11th century and was built in Romanesque style. The simplicity and absence of decoration and the blocks of stone used to build the massive walls are an impressive testimonial to sober military architecture.

The castle is one of the most important sights in Spain, and is the most visited Spanish fortress after the Alhambra (see page 362). The Romanesque church with its barrel vault ceiling occupies the largest surface area in the fortress. The keep, situated behind the church, was used as an assembly room for synods and meetings of the clergy.

The dungeons were cut deep down into the rock. Prisoners were safe down there because they could only get out by means of winches and ropes, so escape was impossible. Stairs from the keep lead to a tunnel that goes to the sea so that the occupants could escape by boat if necessary, or it could be used to keep the fortress supplied with provisions in case of siege. Above the entrance to the keep is the coat-of-arms of Benedict XIII: the papal crown, two keys and a waning moon. Before taking office as antipope, he was called Pedro de Luna, so he was also known as Papa Luna. He was elected in Avignon as the third antipope, on the condition that he would step down to resolve the schism between Avignon and Rome if required. He was asked to do so in 1409, but he refused and continued appointing cardinals. The schism, when two parallel popes claimed authority, lasted from 1371 to 1417. In that year, Papa Luna was deposed by the Council of Constance which ended the Great Schism. Abandoned by his followers and accused of heresy, Benedict fled to Peëíscola. He survived several attempts to poison him and tried, until his death in 1423, to retain his claim to the papacy. The fortress still contains a few memorabilia belonging to Papa Luna.

RIGHT
Peñíscola is one of the most breathtaking of all Spanish castles. Built on a rocky outcrop high above the sea, it looks almost like a fortress within a fortress because the surrounding town itself is also filled with towers, bulwarks and gates ▶

TOWER OF BELÉM

This fortress tower is the architectural symbol of Portugal as well as a World Heritage Site listed by UNESCO. It is also a symbol of the spirit of this seafaring nation, a metaphor for arrival and expectation, adventure and of the longing for new discoveries beyond the horizon.

The *Torre de Belém* at the entrance to the river Tagus was commissioned by King Manuel I in the early 16th century and built by the architect Francisco de Arruda (1515–21). Originally, the tower stood on an island in the middle of the river but because of the river silting up it is now almost on the west bank, to which it is linked by a narrow bridge.

The Torre de Belém consists of two buildings. At the base is a hexagonal bulwark, and above it a rectangular tower. From the sea, the two buildings together look like a large ship. Although massive and built for defensive purposes, the Torre de Belém is elegant and inviting. The tower has Arabian-style twin windows, some projecting, and an upper section smaller than the rest, so that it tapers towards the top. The battlements are symbolically reinforced by shields decorated with crusaders' crosses. Arranged over the four floors of the tower and approached by a spiral staircase are the armory, the king's room with a south-facing Venetian style balcony, the kitchen and dining room, as well as living quarters for the royal entourage.

At the same level as the entrance, behind walls over 11 ft thick, the bulwark contains the casemates with 17 crenels equipped with cannons. Underneath are the storerooms. The Madonna of Belém keeps a watchful eye over it all: she stands under an ornate baldachin in the middle of the terrace with the Infant Jesus in her arms and a bunch of grapes in her hand.

Belém – Lisbon's cultural quarter

Belém, Lisbon's museum suburb near the Tagus estuary, is a must for all visitors to the Portuguese capital. It is a very pleasant place, set in lush greenery, with delightful walks along the river that are a pleasant alternative to the hectic life of the city center. Besides the the Tower of Belém, there is also the Monastery of Hieronymus – now the archeology and ethnology museum. The neighboring new building houses the maritime museum and planetarium, while the Palacio de Belém contains the National Carriage Museum. The Museu de Arte Popular and the Design Museum are also in this region.

RIGHT:
The Torre de Belém was built to protect Lisbon, yet it has an elegant, inviting appearance because of its Arabianstyle windows ▶

QUELUZ

Streets, residential blocks, industrial estates – and then Queluz in the midst of these inhospitable surroundings. A pearl of Portuguese Rococo architecture surrounded by 21st century urban planning, but the little palace is not subdued by it. Small and graceful, light and colorful, fanciful and intricate, time seems to have stood still in the palace of Queluz and its delightful gardens.

The palace of Queluz is situated just 7 miles northwest of the Portuguese capital Lisbon. It was built in 1747 for King Pedro III and his wife Queen Maria, and the monument in the courtyard in front of the palace is dedicated to her. The palace consists of a central building flanked by two wings, arranged around the large courtyard. The original architect was Mateus Vicente de Oliviera, who was replaced in 1760 by the French architect Jean Baptiste Robillon. The classical order of columns and triangular pediment with the imposing coat-of-arms on the central section is lightened by tall windows with very ornate rounded arches, and a balustrade ornamented with figures.

The interior is decorated in a lavish Rococo style with paintings, Gobelin tapestries and elaborate decoration. The Throne Room has gilt stucco walls and allegorical paintings on the ceiling, while the Ambassador's room is decorated with wonderful Chinese wooden panels. Today the music room, lit by magnificent Venetian chandeliers, is used for classical concerts while the Throne Room is also used for concerts, as well as for receptions and balls. The ancient castle kitchen is now a five-star restaurant.

Simple splendor – splendid simplicity

The garden is in the formal French style with straight paths and flowerbeds, enclosed by box hedges. It is enhanced with sculptures and figures. As in all southern gardens, water plays an important part because it is more than just a decorative feature, it is also a source of life. It burbles and reflects the palace and the flowers, as it runs through a canal 165 ft long. Its sides are lined with azulejos, the typical Portuguese tiles, as are the park benches. All these decorative elements, sparkling in the bright southern sun, contribute to the wonderfully light overall impression of the palace and gardens that are summed up in its name: Queluz – "What a light!"

RIGHT
Queluz took its name from the southern light reflected by the pastel facade ▶

FOLLOWING DOUBLE SPREAD
The Hall of Ambassadors in Queluz ▶▶

Glossary

apse	Semi-circular area terminating the nave or chancel of a church or chapel.
arabesque	Decoration of intertwined foliage and tendrils, originally used in Greek and Roman antiquity.
arcade	Construction with a regular succession of openings formed by columns or arches.
bacchantes	Companions of Dionysus, god of the wine.
balcony	Unroofed projecting platform in a wall above ground level with waist-high parapet or columns, sometimes with steps.
balustrade	Handrail supported by columns.
barbican	Outer defense of a castle, usually semi-circular, protecting a gate or tower.
Baroque	Style of architecture, tending to the grandiose, usually symmetrical and decorative, designed to achieve dynamic spatial effects, particularly when combined with painting.
bastion	Structure projecting from the castle wall to carry guns; later arrow-shaped to make it possible to aim in different directions.
battery	Fortified gun emplacement for several guns.
blind arcade	Arcade without openings set against a wall, used as a decorative element.
cap	Conical pitched tower roof.
capital	The top part of a column or a pillar.
cascade	Artificial waterfall running over rocks or steps.
casemate	Individual fortified artillery emplacement.
coffer	Ornamental sunken panel, usually square and often repeated in a ceiling.
colonnades	Row of columns supporting horizontal beams or the upper floors of a building, used on facades, along streets etc.; similar to arcade.
cornice	Horizontal projecting molding applied to a wall or facade.
crossing	The part of a church formed by the intersection of the nave, chancel and transepts, often surmounted by a dome, tower or steeple.
curtain wall	Outer wall enclosing the whole castle. In some castles, this function is performed by the backs of the buildings.
ditch	Ditch outside the walls of a castle.
donjon	Large tower or keep in a medieval castle.
enfilade	Row of rooms aligned so that, if doors are open, the last room can be seen from the first.
entrenchment	Small defensive work with parapet and ditch.
first floor	Floor raised above ground level, normally used for the main reception areas in palaces (also known as the piano nobile).
fluting	Arrangement of concave vertical grooves.
fresco	Wall painting executed on wet plaster; the colors are bonded immovably to the plaster when it is dry.
frieze	Horizontal strip with or without ornamentation at the top part of the wall surface.
gallery	Long room, often extending the whole length of a building,.
Ganerbenburg	German term for a German castle divided up and shared between several families (Ganerben), usually related, living together under formal rules.
grisaille	Monochrome painting, usually gray, but sometimes using greenish or brownish tones.

grotesque	Ornamentation derived from antiquity using fruits, flowers, human and animal forms, often imaginatively distorted.
hammer beam	Beam used in roof construction, one end of which rests on the outside wall with the other supporting a brace and strut.
ideal city	City planned according to aesthetic, geometrical, ornamental and/or sociological principles.
keep	Tall tower of medieval castles, used as a lookout and ultimate refuge against the enemy, not originally residential; usually with a raised entrance reached by a wooden ladder, wooden bridge, or less commonly, a stone stairway.
landscape garden	Style of garden design developed in England in the 18th century under the influence of Romanticism. The objective was to create an artificial landscape of idealized natural appearance, using or changing natural topographical features and arranging trees individually or in clumps, monuments, artificial ruins, temples and pavilions in a harmonious whole.
lantern	Round or polygonal glazed structure set on a dome or roof and letting in light.
lesene	Pilaster strip without base or capital.
lucarne	Small window often richly decorated projecting from a roof.
naiads	In Greek mythology, the nymphs or spirits, of rivers, springs and fountains.
nymphs	Female nature deities of ancient Greek mythology.
outer bailey	The space between outer and inner defense walls, enhancing the defensive function of a castle, particularly before the invention of firearms. It was also used for competitions and as an animal enclosure.
overdoor	Surface above a door with carved or painted decoration.
parterre	Terrace of formal flowerbeds on a level surface.
pendentive	Curved corner surface beneath a dome.
pilaster	Flattened rectangular column with base and capital with no load bearing function, attached to a wall as decoration.
porphyry	Fine or coarse-grained reddish volcanic rock with figuring.
portico	Colonnade, usually projecting with flat or pedimented roof, forming the entrance to a building, typical of classical architecture.
projection	Part of a building advanced from the plane of the main wall, sometimes also higher, such as an entrance bay or corner tower; a common feature of Baroque buildings.
putto, (plural: putti)	Sculpture of naked cherub-like boy, usually with wings.
quatrefoil	Gothic tracery with four symmetrically arranged arcs and cusps.
rampart walk	Walk behind a battlemented parapet.
rampart	Defensive earth or stone wall surrounding a castle; also called a bulwark.
rocaille	The French word literally meaning "rockwork;" used to describe the rock and shell decoration in artificial grottoes.
Rococo	Fanciful late-Baroque decoration, often curved and asymmetrical, based on plants, shells and other natural elements. The word comes from the French rocaille.
rotunda	A circular construction.
skeleton construction	All loadbearing functions are carried by members forming a framework (skeleton) resting on the foundations. The areas between are filled with non-supporting material.
solar	Small usually private room on the first floor approached from the great hall.

strapwork	Decoration element consisting of interlacing bands.
stucco	Malleable, plaster-like mixture of gypsum, sand, water and a binder such as glue, used either smooth or shaped in situ.
stuccowork	Decorative ornament made from stucco, usually applied to walls and ceilings.
tracery	Ornamental effect formed by the curving, branching and interlacing of mullions in Gothic windows and arcades.
turret	Small round tower usually used as a lookout, but sometimes equipped with guns for defense.
vestibule	Anteroom or lobby.
votive picture	A picture donated to a religious place to give thanks for rescue from danger or the answering of prayers, often painted by laymen.

Index of people

Index of places

Acknowledgements

Bayer. Verwaltung der staatlichen Schlösser, Gärten und Seen, Munich: pp 60, 64, 68

A. Bednorz, Cologne: pp 22, 38, 85, 120, 126/127, 171, 172/173, 181, 193, 196, 204, 205, 356, 387, 403

Bildarchiv Monheim, Meerbusch: back cover, middle /Mark Fiennes/ Arcaid: back cover, right pp 2/3, 18, 19, 69, 72, 79, 90/91, 96, 106, 124, 128, 133, 136, 138, 140/141, 149, 150/151, 152, 160/161, 162, 166/167, 168, 186, 187, 215, 219, 226/227, 232, 233, 238/239, 245, 246/247, 248, 257, 258/259, 260, 308, 311, 314, 316/317 /Barbara Opitz: p 180 /Artur/Klaus Frahm: pp 335 /Lisa Hammel: pp 89, 94/95, 323, 330/331, 332 /Robert Janke: pp 24, 26, 184, 202/203 /R. von Götz: pp 304/305

W. Fritz, Cologne: pp 132, 144, 271, 276, 352

R. Kiedrowski, Ratingen: pp 35, 61, 241, 268/269, 359

Laif, Cologne/Anna Neumann: p 326 /F. Zanettini: pp 288, 292, 322 / Gernot Huber: pp 57, 381

Look, Munich/Franz Marc Frei: p. 390 /Hauke Dressler: p 371, /Jürgen Richter: pp 362, 394/395, 401 /Karl Heinz Raach: p. 298 /Karl Johaentges: p. 48 /Rainer Martini: p 338

White Star, Hamburg/Jörg Steinert: pp 380, 391 /Monika Gumm: pp 364/365

E. Wrba, Sulzbach: pp 209, 212/213, 240

Shutterstock: Oscity: front cover leoks: pp 11, 25, 115, 121 / Denis Linine: pp 12, 147 / Inu: pp 13, 184 / macfuton: pp 14, 272 / Peter Probst: pp 14, 340/341 / julian elliott: pp 17, 165 / Oleg Senkov: p 28 / Bonnie Fink: p 29 / D Bond: p 30/31 / vichie81: pp 40/41, 140/141 / Takashi Images: pp 45, 176/177 / Kravtsov_Ivan: p 50 / igor marx: p 52 / Dmitry Eagle Orlov: p 53 / Fexel: p 56 / heiko-neumann-photography: p 58/59 / PM Photostock: back cover, left p62/63 / ABC Photo: p 66/67 / Traveller70: p 75 / VVO: p 78 / Elena Kharichkina: pp 80/81, 82, 86/87 / 360b: p 84 / the_lazy_pigeon: p 88 / Andrey Starostin: p92 / Bildagentur Zoonar GmbH: p 97 / hecke61: p 103 / Andrew Mayovskyy: p 104/105 / Maik Hoehne: p 108, 112 / Millionstock.com: p 118 / Jorg Hackemann: p 122/123 / Tatiana Popova: p 130 / Boris Stroujko: p 131 / posztos: p 138 / Vladimir Korostyshevskiy: p 139 / Kiev.Victor: pp 142, 192, 266 / Natali Glado: p 146 / Pierre Jean Durieu: p 155 / Tomsickova Tatyana: p 159 / Duncan Gilbert: p 164 / PHB.cz (Richard Semik): p 188/189 / ThomasLENNE: p 194/195 / Julia700702: p 208 / villorejo: p 216 / Paul Wishart: p 222 / PlusONE: p 225 / Christophe Cappelli: p228 / Edward Haylan: p 234/235 / chrisdorney: p 242 / GTS Productions: p 262, 339 / Valery Egorov: p 264/265, 329 / macfuton: p 272 / Jeffrey B. Banke: p 274/275 / Rob Crandall: p 281 / Stefan Holm: p 283, 286 / Kravtsov_Ivan: p 289 / TTstudio: 290/291, 328 / Oliver Foerstner: 296/297 / Mike Mareen: p 302/303 / Art Konovalov: p 310 / Iakov Filimonov: 312/313 / janprchal: p 318 / Petr Podrouzek: p 320/321 / Peter Probst: p 340/341 / Alberto Masnovo: p 342 / vvoe: p 343 / Joost van Uffelen: p 348 /
Songquan Deng: p 349 / massimhokuto: p 354/355 / Javier_Rejon: p 363 / Fotografiecor.nl: p 366/367 / fz-foto: p 368/369 / Renata Sedmakova: p 370 / joan_bautista: p 372 / Jose Ignacio Soto: p374/375 / felipe caparros: p 376 / Atalis: p 386 / Loredana Cirstea: p 388/389 / Lepneva Irina: p 392/393 / bimserd: p 398/399

Dreamstime: Markus Gann: pp 1, 36-37 / Marlee: pp 10, 378 / Tobias Arhelger: p 20 / Karel gallors: p 32 / Sapientisat: p 39, 42 / Xantana: p 51 / Dmitry Fedyaev: p 54 / Somchai Sinthop: p 70/71 / Anatolii Lyzun: p 85 / Ivan Kravtsov: p 98/99 / Hecke01: p 100 / Sarkao: p 114 / Moniciu: p 145 / Jana Gardianova: p 175 / Ams22: p 178 / Richard Semik: p 190 / Petr Švec: p 198/199 / Anthony Shaw Photography: p 201 / Yuliya Heikens: p 210/211 / Saphire Ovadia: p 218 / Chris Doyle: p 220/221 / Steve Allen: p 236 / Tosca Weijers: p 240 / Pepperboxdesign: p 251 / Leigh Norris: p 252/253 / Richard Billingham: p 254 / David Lloyd: p 267 / Areinwald: p 268/269 /
Lanceb: p 270 / Creativehearts: p 273 / Peter Helin: p 279 / Cellai Stefano: p 284/285 / Ciolca: p 294 / Pytyczech: p 301 / Grigory Evdokimov: p 306 / Dmitriy Raykin: p 307 / Andrey Andronov: p 324/325 / minnystock: p 336/337 / Anilah: p 344 / Boggy: p 345 / photogolfer: p 346 / Andrei Stancu: p 347 / Fabrizio Argonauta: p 353 / Ciolca: p 358 / Madrugadaverde: pp 379, 397 / Jose I. Soto: p 382/383, 406/407 / Finadiz: p 384 / Michael Warwick: 405

Adobestock: Klaus Büth: p 46/47 / Sydney2000: p 76/77 / Jens Hofmann: p 110/111 / patron74: p 116/117 / franke182: p 134/135 / pigprox: p 154 / pictarena: p 156/157 / Vermeulen-Perdaen: p 206/207 / sandroguidelli:p 230/231 / Lance Bellers: p 263 / anilah: p 359 / NoraDoa: p 373

Detlef Huhn via Wiki Commons: p 109

The publisher thanks Bayerischen Verwaltung der staatlichen Schlösser, Gärten und Seen, Munich, for making available photographs of Schloss Neuschwanstein, Schloss Linderhof and Schloss Nymphenburg.